your PERSONALITY QUIZ BOOK

your PERSONALITY
QUIZ BOOK

Find out what makes you tick

Dr Glenn Wilson · top psychologist

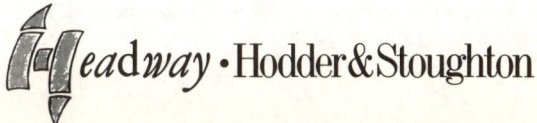

Headway · Hodder & Stoughton

British Library Cataloguing in Publication Data

Wilson, Glenn
  Your Personality Quiz Book
  I. Title
  155.2

  ISBN 0 340 60486 7

First published 1994
Impression number 10 9 8 7 6 5 4 3 2 1
Year   1999   1998   1997   1996   1995   1994

Typeset by Rowland Phototypesetting Limited, Bury St Edmunds, Suffolk.
Printed in Great Britain for Hodder & Stoughton Educational,
a division of Hodder Headline Plc, 338 Euston Road, London NW1 3BH
by Cox & Wyman Ltd, Reading, Berks.

CONTENTS

PREFACE

'Be yourself' is good advice for, as Walt Disney observed, 'you can't be anybody else'. But in order to be yourself it is first necessary to *know* yourself, and this is easier said than done.

Many people think they know themselves inside out – after all they have lived with themselves all their life – and, indeed, they may know many things about themselves that they have revealed to no-one. But what they perhaps lack is an outside perspective and a proper comparison with the thoughts, feelings and behavioural style of other people. This is the kind of self-knowledge that questionnaires can provide. They enable us to compare ourselves with other people. The biggest mistake we can make is to use ourselves as a model to the extent that we assume everybody else is just the same – for the differences between individuals are quite profound.

The quizzes in this book are intended to provide you with amusement as well as some insight into your personality, attitudes, preferences and potential. They may even help you to develop your understanding of other people, your social skills, your sense of humour, your sexual knowledge and your relationships. This may happen as you examine the response options and read the comments about their meaning. Sometimes, one alternative may seem more adjusted or 'healthy' than another. However, there are no 'right' or 'wrong' answers to most of the questions, and you will find the book most useful if you answer them honestly and thus discover whom you 'really' are.

Some of the questions may seem impossible to answer for some reason. For example, they might assume you drive a car when you do not, or are appropriate to women rather than men. Do not get hung up on any problems like this: just do the best you can to give some kind of answer that would represent your attitude if you were in that position. The scoring systems work on broad patterns of answers, so no one response is going to matter all that much. It is best if you work quickly and do not ponder each individual question too much. Your first reaction is usually the most valid one.

Each quiz has a brief introduction describing its purpose and is followed by scoring instructions and some notes for interpretation and guidance for possible improvement. The material is light-hearted and geared to entertainment as well as self-exploration; hence it should not be taken too seriously. Although devised in the light of established psychological principles, these tests do not conform to strict psychometric criteria, such as norms based on large population samples or specific validation against external criteria. Therefore, if major life decisions such as changing jobs or marriage partners are contemplated, they should not be based on these results. Professional counselling should be sought, or more thorough and reliable testing by a Chartered Psychologist.

Enjoy yourself, learn about yourself, but do not get suicidal or throw yourself into precipitous lifestyle changes on the strength of the results. After all, you may just have added up the scores incorrectly!

I

YOUR PERSONALITY: MAJOR

TEMPERAMENTAL TRAITS

How do you see yourself, and how do others see you? For many of us there is a mighty gulf between our own self-concept and the way we are viewed by other people. You may regard yourself as painfully shy and doubt-ridden, while others see you as outgoing and brimming with confidence. You may think of yourself as totally stable, while others see you as a candidate for the 'funny farm'. You may think of yourself as gentle, sensitive and altruistic, while others see you as aggressively self-interested and grasping.

The quiz below will go some way towards enabling us to see ourselves as others see us. First answer the questions for yourself, then have somebody else who knows you well answer them on your behalf. The differences between your own replies and those that your friends think you should have given may be quite revealing.

The quiz is in three parts, corresponding to three major personality dimensions identified by world-famous psychologist Hans J. Eysenck. These are three of the main ways in which people differ one from another. The meaning of these three dimensions is summarised, along with the scoring procedure, at the end of the quiz.

In answering the questions, force yourself to say 'yes' or 'no' to each, however difficult it may be to decide. Be honest, but do not worry too much about the precise meaning of any one item: it is the overall pattern that counts and there are no right or wrong answers.

When you have finished, ask a friend to answer the questions for you, in the way they think you *should* have answered them if you were being totally candid – without letting that friend see what your actual answers were. It is best if you put your answers on separate sheets of paper so that your and your friend's replies do not bias each other.

EXTROVERT OR INTROVERT?

1 Do you become restless when working at something in which there is little action?   *Yes   No*

2 Do you often try to find the underlying motives for the actions of other people?   *Yes   No*

3 Do you like talking to people so much that you never miss a chance of talking to a stranger?   *Yes   No*

4 If you were making a business enquiry, would you rather write than discuss it on the telephone?   *Yes   No*

5 Are you usually among the last to stop clapping after the end of a concert or stage performance?   *Yes   No*

6 Would you enjoy working on a project that involved a great deal of library research?   *Yes   No*

7 Do you find that you have often crossed a road leaving your more careful companions on the other side?   *Yes   No*

8 Do you wish that you were able to 'let yourself go' and have a good time more often?   *Yes   No*

9 Do you need to use a lot of self-control to keep out of trouble?   *Yes   No*

10 Would you always be careful to declare everything at the customs if you had travelled abroad?   *Yes   No*

EMOTIONAL OR STABLE?

1 Do you often lose sleep over your worries?   *Yes   No*

2 In general, would you say you are satisfied with your life?   *Yes   No*

3 Are you sometimes bothered by an unimportant thought that runs through your mind for days?   *Yes   No*

4 Do you see your future as looking quite bright?   *Yes   No*

5   Are you often afraid of things and people that you know would not really hurt you?   *Yes   No*

6   Do you have a great deal of confidence in your decisions?   *Yes   No*

7   Do you often feel ashamed of things that you have done?   *Yes   No*

8   Do you smile and laugh as much as most people?   *Yes   No*

9   Do you get very upset if someone criticises you?   *Yes   No*

10   Do you think it is a waste of time going to the doctor with most mild complaints such as coughs, colds and flu?   *Yes   No*

TOUGH OR TENDER?

1   If someone does you a bad turn do you feel obliged to do something about it?   *Yes   No*

2   Do you set your aspirations low in order to avoid disappointments?   *Yes   No*

3   Do you get very angry when you read what certain politicians have said in the newspaper?   *Yes   No*

4   Do you often question your own morality and rules of conduct?   *Yes   No*

5   Do you like scenes of violence and torture in the movies?   *Yes   No*

6   Are you 'turned off' by crude and vulgar jokes?   *Yes   No*

7   Do you sometimes do slightly dangerous things 'just for the hell of it'?   *Yes   No*

8   Do you find it difficult to resist picking up and cuddling small furry animals?   *Yes   No*

9   Does your blood boil when people stubbornly refuse to admit they are wrong?   *Yes   No*

10 Would you put yourself out a great deal to help
somebody who was suffering an emotional hurt?   *Yes   No*

SCORING

Extravert or introvert

Give yourself one point for each 'yes' to questions 1, 3, 5, 7 and 9, and
one point for each 'no' answer to questions 2, 4, 6, 8 and 10.

If you scored 8–10 you are an extravert, which means outgoing,
sociable, active and impulsive.

If you scored 0–2 you are an introvert – quiet, controlled, thoughtful
and responsible.

A score of 3–7 means that you are ambivert – sharing some of the
characteristics of each of the other types.

Because high scores have been attached to the extravert end of the
dimension, this does not mean it is necessarily better to be an extravert. Extraverted people may be happier and more fun to be with, but
introverts tend to be more independent and reliable. Therefore, both
types have their merits.

Emotional or stable

Give yourself one point for each 'yes' to questions 1, 3, 5, 7 and 9, and
one point for each 'no' to questions 2, 4, 6, 8 and 10.

8–10 means you are highly emotional – inclined to be anxious,
depressed, fearful, guilt-ridden and generally harried by life.

0–2 means you are unusually stable – confident, secure and
untroubled by events.

3–7 indicates a fairly average degree of emotionality. You are reasonably well-adjusted, but not totally immune to worrying.

Because high scores have been attached to the extravert end of the
dimension, this does not mean it is necessarily better to be an extravert. Extraverted people may be happier and more fun to be with, but
introverts tend to be more independent and reliable. Therefore, both
types have their merits.

Tough or tender

Score one for each 'yes' to questions 1, 3, 5, 7 and 9, and one for each 'no' to questions 2, 4, 6, 8 and 10.

8–10 puts you at the tough end of the dimension – assertive, aggressive, ambitious and sensation-seeking.

0–2 means you are very tender-minded – kind, considerate, empathetic and nurturant.

3–7 puts you in the average range – a mixture of tough and tender characteristics.

Again, both types of people are valuable to society. Tough people 'get ahead' in life and get things done, while tender people provide support, companionship and consolation. Needless to say, there is a sex difference on this attribute – men tend to be tougher on average, and women more tender, but there is considerable overlap between the genders.

After you have scored your personality as reported by yourself, use the same system for scoring the replies your friend has given on your behalf. You may then discover that whereas you think of yourself as introvert, emotional and tender, your friend sees you as extrovert, stable and tough. Such a discrepancy is reasonably common because we are often more aware of our own uncertainties and emotional conflicts than are other people. There are, however, many other possible combinations.

In interpreting these differences, you need to consider the possibility that one or both of you did not give honest answers. In particular, your friend might feel inhibited about saying ungenerous things about you. A discussion about how honest you both were might clarify the true position. If you are still not satisfied, find some more people to rate your personality.

When you have finished the analysis of your own personality, you might like to swap roles, so that your friend becomes the object of scrutiny. Try to avoid the temptation of using this as an opportunity for counter-complimentation or revenge.

2

WHAT ARE YOUR EMOTIONAL

NEEDS?

All of us have needs, and much of our day-to-day behaviour is devoted to satisfying them. In Western society, most of us go to work each day in order to earn the necessary amount of money to take care of physical needs such as food, shelter and clothing. But we have other needs that are a major motivational factor directing our dealings with other people and our preferences among different types of work and leisure activities.

Psychologists use the importance of various needs as a way of classifying personality. Most of us like to socialise with other people (affiliation need), to get on in the world (achievement need), to be looked after by other people (nurturance need), to gain and wield power over others (dominance need), to experience new and interesting things (novelty need), and so on. Various lists have been compiled by different psychologists. Although all of these things are desired by nearly all of us to some extent, it is the priorities we put upon them that are used as the basis for personality description.

The quiz that follows will help you to assess your own position with respect to three major psychological needs that have been found by research to lend structure to the social, sexual and general behaviour of people. It is laid out in such a way that although you might think all options appeal to you, you are bound to make choices, and these preferences will give clues as to your personality.

I The main impression you set out to make on the opposite sex is that you:

   a Would give them a secure future and happy home life.

   b Would always be a source of creativity and inspiration to them.

  c Could introduce them to more excitement and sensual
delight than they dreamed possible.

2 Which city would you choose to live in?

  a Boston or Copenhagen, where life is generally ordered and
restful.
  b Paris or London, where culture and the arts are foremost.
  c Tel Aviv or Beirut, where there is an air of unrest and the
uncertainty of potential war.

3 What kind of future do we owe our children?

  a A responsible, pollution-free environment.
  b A heritage, rich in culture and history.
  c A genuinely free-thinking, permissive society.

4 On a cold winter's evening, do you like to:

  a Curl up in front of the fire with your lover?
  b Engage in heated political discourse with friends?
  c Go to see the hottest new group in town?

5 Most of your friends are:

  a Respectable and hard-working.
  b Eccentric academics or artists.
  c Fun-loving hedonists.

6 Which club would you join?

  a The Rotary or similar, doing good works in the
neighbourhood.
  b The Byron Society, or one which kept alive the works of
great writers.
  c Skin-Two, where you are required to dress outrageously in
leather or rubber and enact diverse sexual fantasies.

7 You feel most restricted if you are deprived of:

  a Your credit cards.
  b Your books.
  c Your passport.

8 You want the place you live in to:

  a Be a secure and peaceful 'haven'.
  b Immerse you in a cultural climate.
  c Be somewhere to store necessities until you move on.

9 Your ideal holiday would be:

    a In a luxury hotel with a view.

    b On an island, rich in ancient or primitive archeological ruins.

    c Trekking through the Amazon jungle with a native guide.

10 For a friend's birthday you would buy them:

    a Something useful for the home.

    b A fascinating book.

    c Something exotic and unusual.

11 Your main goal in life is to:

    a Make a successful marriage.

    b Expand your mind to its maximum potential.

    c Live every second to the full.

12 Ideally, you prefer your day to:

    a Follow the same pattern.

    b Offer the opportunity to learn something new.

    c Be filled with novel and stimulating experiences.

13 What are you best at?

    a Making strangers feel at ease.

    b Conversing intelligently on almost any subject.

    c Throwing sensational parties.

14 You could go without sleep for a long time if:

    a You were nursing a sick child or relative.

    b You were engrossed in an interesting project.

    c You were involved in a dare-devil task.

15 What type of car do you (or would you be inclined to) drive?

    a A comfortable saloon car with plenty of room in the boot.

    b A battered old model which gets you from A to B.

    c A snazzy sports car with electronic gadgets.

16 You love the smell of:

    a Fresh-baked bread.

    b Musty old buildings.

    c Burning incense.

17 Your favourite alcoholic drink is:

   a Sweet sherry.
   b Vintage French wine.
   c Fancy cocktails.

18 You enjoy watching:

   a A favourite TV programme.
   b A witty parliamentary debate.
   c People sky-diving off high cliffs.

19 Which radio station do you listen to the most?

   a Radio 2 – familiar records and friendly DJs.
   b Radio 3 – classical recitals and discussions.
   c Radio 1 – popular music.

20 You would be flattered if someone described you as:

   a A kind, caring person.
   b Extremely bright and forward-thinking.
   c Wacky and spirited.

SCORING

Add up the number of 'a', 'b' and 'c' responses that you gave to give three scores out of 20. Now interpret these scores as follows:

Mostly 'a's

Your dominant need is for *security*. This means that you have a liking for things that are familiar rather than novel, comfortable rather than exciting, safe rather than dangerous, and stable rather than changeable. Some people might call you conservative, though in this context they would mean conservative with a small 'c', in other words, they think of you as a person who is moderate or cautious in outlook, and who is reluctant to consider new ideas.

Naturally, nearly everybody likes some degree of security, but your high score on this category suggests that you set a higher premium on security than other needs, such as fun and curiosity.

As with almost any personality trait, there are positive and negative sides. Most obviously, you are unlikely to throw away your life in some reckless adventure and you are unlikely to endanger the lives of other people. As a driver, for example, you are probably very considerate and safe and you no doubt take good care of your family, informing them of dangers, taking out full insurance policies, and so on. As a partner you are probably also regarded as stable, loyal and supportive. On the debit side, some people might view you as staid, even boring, and as you perhaps already appreciate, there is a possibility that you are missing out on some of the colour and thrills of life.

Mostly 'b's

Your primary need is for *intellectual and cultural stimulation*. You are the sort of person who would be happy living in a big town.

Your interest in people is not so much motivated by the need for emotional attachment or companionship as such, as by the desire to exchange ideas and information concerning cultural events. You are likely to be an avid patron of libraries, museums, theatres, institutions of higher learning, quality newspapers and factual TV documentaries.

Your best attribute might be your ability to converse intelligently on a wide variety of different issues which would make you interesting company at parties and as a long-term companion. On the negative side, some people complain that 'culture vultures' lack real warmth and humanity and that their profound ponderings are the exact opposite to fun and frolics.

Mostly 'c's

Your primary need is for *sensuous excitement*. You are hedonistic, adventurous and determined that life is to be experienced to the full. In many ways your preference is opposite to that of the security-seeker, but you are opposite to the culture-seeker in a different respect – you put a premium on sensual stimulation while he/she seeks intellectual titillation.

You are no doubt good fun to go around with and therefore have lots of friends, and you seldom have cause to regret the experiences you have missed out on. Your critics might say that you are a danger to yourself and others, that you are shallow (if not empty) and that you are unreliable, irresponsible and disloyal when it comes to social and marital attachments. As with the other categories, there is probably some truth to both the pro and con sides of your personality; few personality traits can be regarded as universally good or bad.

3

ARE YOU A MORNING OR AN

EVENING PERSON?

Some people are at their peak of efficiency the moment their eyelids open in the morning. Others are slow to warm up and cannot function until several hours (and several cups of coffee) later. The latter are likely to be night owls flourishing well after dark when the early birds are settling down to sleep. Neither is necessarily any better at 'getting the worm', but it may help to be clear about where your own optimum lies within the daily cycle so you can plan important events accordingly. Discover your 'diurnal dynamics' by answering these questions.

1   What is the first thing you do in the morning?

    a Check to see if you are still alive.
    b Make a cup of tea or coffee.
    c Leap out of bed and do your exercises.

2   What words would you be most likely to utter on waking to brilliant sunshine?

    a 'Oh God, not another sunny day.'
    b 'Looks like it's going to be a fine day.'
    c 'Oh, what a beautiful morning.'

3   If you were staying in a hotel, what would you order for breakfast?

    a Breakfast – yuk! You never touch it.
    b A 'continental' breakfast.
    c All the yummy things you don't have time to cook at home.

4   What is your best time for getting constructive work done?

    a You can't function at all before midday.

b It depends how much you have to do.

c You leap into action bright and early.

5 If you were going for a job interview, when would you make your best impression?

a After a sauna and a visit to the hairdresser.

b Just after lunch when your prospective boss is hopefully mellow.

c At the first appointment of the day.

6 If you were invited to a cocktail party after work on a weekday, you would:

a Jump at the opportunity – you really sparkle in the happy hour.

b Pop in for a while just to be sociable.

c Decline – you feel too exhausted after work to change for a party.

7 Which would be your ideal date?

a A dance that goes on till the early hours.

b A lavish picnic by a lake.

c A champagne breakfast.

8 When do you most enjoy making love?

a In the dark when you feel naughty.

b When the mood takes you.

c When you are rested and fresh.

9 How do you sleep at night?

a There is no point in going to bed before midnight – you couldn't get to sleep anyway.

b Better if you don't have a heavy meal or drink coffee.

c You are liable to nod off at any time after supper – the problem is trying to stay awake if you have a social engagement at night.

10 Providing the pay was the same, which would you apply for as a part-time job?

a A croupier in a casino.

b A receptionist.

c A trendy market stall-holder.

11 You prefer to go shopping:

    a At supermarkets that stay open late.
    b When it's most convenient to you.
    c With an early start, when the shelves are freshly stocked.

12 What is your favourite type of fragrance?

    a Exotic and musky.
    b Woody and ferny.
    c Fresh and floral.

13 Which of these sensations appeals most to you?

    a The neon lights of theatreland.
    b Fully-opened flowers.
    c The sound of birds singing at daybreak.

14 If you were to take up jogging on a regular basis, when would you probably do it?

    a After tea in the evening.
    b Lunchtime or afternoon.
    c Before work in the morning.

15 When looking for a new house or flat, in which direction would you prefer to face?

    a West.
    b North or south.
    c East.

16 What colours would you choose to decorate your lounge?

    a Deep, dark dramatic tones, such as wine red or navy blue.
    b Practical, natural colours, such as green and brown.
    c Light and bright pastel shades, such as primrose yellow or powder pink.

17 Suppose you were given £300 to spend on one outfit. Which would you buy?

    a A glamorous evening gown.
    b A fur coat, marked down in a sale.
    c An extremely chic 'designer' suit.

18 Which type of music do you prefer?

    a Cool jazz.

    b Classical symphonies.
    c Brass band marches.

19   If your best friend wanted to pour his/her heart out, when should they phone you for a good reception?

    a At the end of the day when you could lend a sympathetic ear.
    b Anytime – that's what friends are for.
    c Before you leave for work.

20   If you went abroad on holiday by plane, what would be your favourite view on landing?

    a The resort ablaze with lights.
    b Looking down on a sun-drenched beach.
    c A panoramic view of the rising sun.

SCORING

Give yourself 3 points for each 'a' answer, 2 points for each 'b', and 1 for each 'c'. This should give you a total score of something between 20 and 60.

Score: 50–60

You are in the night-owl category, shunning the daylight and coming into your own after sundown. This is no problem if you work in the evenings, but it must be hell if you have to start work at 9 am. Remember that these daily cycles are fixed by habit as much as by nature, so you can, if you wish, adjust your lifestyle so as to peak earlier. If you have trouble getting to sleep before midnight, avoid coffee after midday and engage in some strenuous exercise, such as jogging or skipping, around 9 or 10 pm.

Score: 30–49

You may be gratified to know that you are normal – capable of adjusting fairly easily either to a daytime or night-time existence. You too may like to note that truly restful sleep is obtained with good food, exercise and fresh air, not stimulants or sleeping pills.

Score: 20—29

You are the original early bird, which is ideal provided you do not work a night shift. More likely you have discovered the secret of good living, which someone once defined (somewhat ambiguously) as 'early to bed and up with the cock'. Seriously though, the morning can be an especially beautiful time which, in this increasingly nocturnal world, you can savour almost in solitude.

4

HOW TACTFUL ARE YOU?

Are you the soul of discretion, sparing the feelings of others as far as possible, and acting with complete diplomacy at all times? Or, are you brutally frank and forthright in criticism, proud of your cutting line of invective; not the one to suffer fools gladly? Whether for the sake of others, or the furtherance of your own relationships and professional career, tact is an important social grace that is well worth acquiring if it does not come naturally. Answer the quiz below to assess your current standing with respect to this virtue.

I Someone you find distinctly unattractive makes an amorous proposition. You would say:

   a 'Go bury yourself – I wouldn't consider you if you were the last person on earth.'

   b 'Sorry, I'm busy that night – and every other night.'

   c 'Thanks, but my love-life is very full at the moment.'

2 A friend has just been to the hairdresser and comes out looking ghastly. You would say:

   a 'You look dreadful – you ought to sue.'

   b 'They've cut it too short, but it won't take long to grow again.'

   c 'How nice to see you, have you just been to the hairdresser?'

3 You see an elderly person in a supermarket absentmindedly put something in their pocket instead of their basket. You would:

   a Report them immediately to the manager for shoplifting.

   b Take no notice and go about your business.

   c Gently point out their mistake to save embarrassment.

4 You are at a dinner party where the food is inedible. You would:

   a Proclaim your disgust at the top of your voice.

   b Push your plate to one side after a couple of mouthfuls.

   c Take pains to compliment your host on anything you *can* eat.

5 Supposing someone you knew quite well had a serious accident and their spouse had to be informed. You would:

   a Think it's a job for the police.

   b Phone one of their relatives and ask them to break the news.

   c Notify them immediately, if possible in person.

6 What would you tell a good friend who had bad breath?

   a They have foul breath that stinks.

   b They must have been eating some pretty strong garlic.

   c Mention casually you have just discovered a fabulous new toothpaste that makes your teeth super shiny.

7 You go to see a friend's teenage children in a school play that turns out to be a crashing bore. You would:

   a Storm out at the interval and demand a refund.

   b Offer some criticism, making allowance for the amateur nature of the performance.

   c Say they played their parts well – you can't see much point in being destructive.

8 Your partner has just returned from an overseas trip. You would:

   a Demand a present.

   b Ask them if they had a good trip.

   c Prepare something special to welcome them home.

9 If you received a present from a relative that was in dreadful taste, would you:

   a Tell them you think it is hideous?

   b Put it in a drawer and never use it?

   c Thank them politely and get a credit note from the shop where they bought it?

10 You are with a disabled person in company with people who are making jokes rather too 'near the knuckle'. You:

   a Relate the 'sickest' story of all.

   b Leave the room.

   c Steer the conversation around to another topic.

11 You are meeting prospective in-laws for the first time. With which of the following would you seek to impress them?

   a Your most expensive outfit.
   b Your academic qualifications.
   c Your charm and warmth of personality.

12 If you were going to a restaurant and you knew one of the people in your group didn't have much money, where would you go?

   a To an expensive restaurant – let them find the money somehow.
   b To a medium-priced restaurant which most people could afford.
   c To a cheap but good, 'fun' restaurant with lots of atmosphere which everyone would enjoy.

13 If you saw a married friend in a passionate embrace with someone other than their spouse, would you:

   a Charge over and slap their face.
   b Warn them that if it happens again you will 'tell'.
   c Pretend you had not seen them – it's not your business.

14 If a neighbour's dog constantly fouled on your doorstep, would you:

   a Pour petrol on the step so the animal would get burnt paws?
   b Say you will report them to the health authority if it happens again?
   c Ask them nicely to please keep the dog on a lead or train it to use the gutter?

15 If a friend had come to a party at your house and, somewhat the worse for drink, was going to drive home, what would you do?

   a Suggest they have 'one more for the road'.
   b Leave them to it – if they want to risk it, it's their own decision.
   c Offer to drive them home or order them a taxi suggesting that they leave their car for collection the next day.

16 When speaking to a client at work on the telephone and you discover they have a bad stammer, would you:

a Lose your temper and tell them to 'spit it out'?

b Try to speed up the conversation by finishing their words for them?

c Show patience and understanding and avoid the temptation to 'put words in their mouth'?

17 You work with someone who constantly talks about themselves. You:

a Tell them you are sick to death of their one-sided monologues.

b Jokingly suggest they 'put a sock in it'.

c Get them interested in other people and projects to distract them from their egotism.

18 You go to see a friend's new baby which is rather ugly. Would you:

a Say it's a pity the baby wasn't around when good looks were being handed out?

b Avoid mentioning the baby at all?

c Congratulate them and say what a lovely character the baby has?

19 You invite a friend to a restaurant (where you are known) for dinner and discover you have left your wallet at home. You:

a Ask them to pay since you have no cash.

b Leave them as 'hostage' while you rush home to collect your wallet.

c Discreetly arrange with the manager to pay the next day.

20 You are walking out of a supermarket and someone in front of you drops her groceries all over the footpath. You:

a Have a good laugh at their expense.

b Pretend you haven't noticed so as to lessen their humiliation.

c Make a light-hearted crack about 'distributing to the poor' and help them by picking up a few things.

SCORING

Give yourself 2 points for each 'c' answer and 1 point for each 'b'. The 'a' answer rates zero in each case. Now add up your total score and interpret it as follows:

Score: 30–40

You appear to be a very tactful person, considerate of other people's feelings, and socially astute in your dealings with them. You could have a career in public relations or as a diplomat.

Score: 20–29

This is the range of scores obtained by average people answering the questions honestly. You have the capacity to be tactful, but every so often you betray a naïve streak or your annoyance gets the better of you and you say or do something that in retrospect you realise might have been unnecessarily frank and hurtful.

Score: 10–19

You are either deficient in social skill or else immune to concern for the feelings of other people. Perhaps you mistakenly believe that open honesty is a central virtue that overrides all other considerations. If so, think back to occasions when your own feelings have suffered as a result of the outspokenness of others, and see if you think they might have been a little more discreet.

Score: 0–9

Perhaps you were joking when you gave your answers. If not, you appear to be a rather rude and boorish person. If you imagine you have any friends at the moment, you may not have for much longer. If they stay your friends, they are either thick-skinned, or just plain thick!

5

HOW IMAGINATIVE ARE YOU?

Are you a free and creative spirit, playful in imagination and fond of fantasy? Or are you realistic and practical in your general approach to life? Some people have an orthodox, straightforward attitude to their daily lifestyle, while others, whom Edward De Bono would call 'lateral thinkers', typically adopt an oblique and unpredictable tack. The former are dependable, if somewhat dull, and the latter are exciting, if sometimes infuriating. Find out how willing you are to let your mind play by answering the following questions.

1 When you look through a kaleidoscope what do you see?

   a A myriad of fantastic settings with outlines of mythical figures.

   b A lot of tiny pieces of coloured glass.

   c Pretty coloured shapes with light shining through.

2 When you have young children in your care, what is top of your list of priorities?

   a Playing games to stimulate their imagination and make them laugh.

   b Seeing that they are disciplined and properly behaved.

   c Keeping them clean and away from danger.

3 Which of the following would you buy as a 'country home' or weekend retreat?

   a A rambling old mansion house with a maze of corridors and vast rooms.

   b A cute little bungalow on a new housing estate.

   c A time-share apartment in a luxury hotel.

4 Suppose you could adopt an animal in the zoo and go to visit it regularly. Which would you choose?

   a A black panther.

b A guinea pig.
c An elephant.

5 What sort of people do you like to have as friends?

a Zany, fun-loving types who are unpredictable.
b Honest, 'salt-of-the-earth' folk who won't let you down in a crisis.
c Wealthy, well-known people who are 'useful'.

6 Which piece of music would you select to enhance your love-making?

a Wagner's *Gotterdamerung* – mind-blowing passion and sweeping plateaus.
b Debussy's *La Mer* – a sweet, romantic piece to soothe and relax you.
c Ravel's *Bolero* – a steady, repetitive pulse that builds in intensity.

7 If you were going on a long plane journey with your lover, you would:

a Stuff a bag full of exciting goodies to surprise and delight them.
b Take a sleeping pill.
c Buy a book at the airport.

8 If your lover wanted to give you a ring, you would choose:

a A modern, futuristic but not very practical design from an art jeweller.
b The most popular design from a well-known high street jeweller.
c A traditional design in an antique setting.

9 If you were having friends to dinner, you would:

a Experiment with at least one dish which is exotic and unusual.
b Always serve a roast and two veg.
c Stick to a recipe which is tried and true.

10 You have a really tedious and repetitive task to do. You:

a Try to recall romantic and amusing incidents to keep you awake.

b Accept that certain things have to be done and you can't expect work to be a hobby.

c Knuckle down and complete the job as soon as possible.

11 What eating plan would you choose to lose weight?

a Turn mundane and diet foods (like raw fruit and vegetables) into a visual feast.

b Cut out starch and sugar.

c Count calories at meal times.

12 Suppose you were given a present of a spectacular make-up box with dozens of assorted colours. You would:

a Create 'faces' to suit your changing moods.

b Give it to someone else – you always wear the same brand and colour of make-up.

c Experiment to find what suited you best and then stick with those colours.

13 When you are making love, you:

a Invent games to please and tease your lover.

b Always wait for your lover to take the initiative.

c Occasionally suggest trying a room other than the bedroom.

14 If you can't get to sleep, do you:

a Close your eyes and drift into a world of fantasy?

b Meticulously count sheep?

c Have a hot drink and think consciously about relaxing your body?

15 What type of gardens do you most enjoy?

a Jungly and overgrown, with waterfalls and rockery.

b Neat, trimmed flower borders and lawns.

c Lots of trees and hedges.

16 Which of these games do you prefer?

a Dungeons and dragons.

b Scrabble.

c Monopoly.

17 What sort of novel would you borrow from the library?

a A raunchy adventure with lots of action and scandal.

   b A reminiscence of childhood and growing up.
   c A romantic love story.

18   In a cocktail bar, you would choose to drink:

   a A long, slow comfortable screw up against the wall.
   b Gin and tonic.
   c Pina colada.

19   Which type of TV programme would you prefer to watch?

   a A Walt Disney cartoon.
   b A family quiz show.
   c An American 'cop' movie.

20   Which of these proverbs best sums up your attitude to money?

   a 'In for a penny, in for a pound'.
   b 'Look after the pennies and the pounds will look after themselves'.
   c 'Penny wise, pound foolish'.

SCORING

Total up the number of 'a', 'b' and 'c' replies that you have given, separately.

Mostly 'a's

You are a creative and imaginative person. Like the Duke of Plaza Toro in Gilbert and Sullivan's *Gondoliers*, you do not follow fashion – you lead it. The mundane is not for you; you like to bring a playful element and excitement into everything you do. Always daring to be different, you get yourself into quite a few scrapes with your unconventional attitude. Occasionally, your 'gad-fly' personality and individualism may irritate other people. If you wonder why people sometimes overreact to you, you might try taking a cool look at your words and actions and adopt a more acceptable attitude to life.

Mostly 'b's

You are an orderly and respectable person, but possibly a bit too concerned about doing the right thing at the right time and having everything in its place. Do not bottle up your feelings because, in the long run, this can lead to an increase in tension and anxiety. It would probably do you good to let your hair down once in a while and experiment with new ideas. Keep an open mind and you could find yourself having a lot more fun than you do at present.

Mostly 'c's

You do have a spark of fun in you, though you go with the tide in the main and will often dine out on someone else's efforts and ideas. Basically a rather conventional soul, you would like to appear more creative. Do not be a slave to fashion, but allow yourself freedom to invent and implement your own original ideas.

6

ARE YOU A RISK TAKER?

Some people put a high premium on safety and security; others will 'chance it' for the big reward, possibly even enjoying the adrenalin 'buzz' that accompanies danger and suspense. Which type are you? Careful, risky, or the balanced, intermediate sort of person? Answer these questions and find out.

1   What would you consider to be your ideal job offer?

   a A steady, salaried position with a pension scheme.
   b A job with considerable independence and opportunity for self-improvement.
   c A crazy dream-scheme that could make you a millionaire if it pays off.

2   Do you feel most comfortable in the company of people who wear:

   a Suits?
   b Casuals?
   c Leather?

3   When you go to a new restaurant, which of the following would you choose to eat?

   a Something you know you like.
   b You might try a new-sounding starter.
   c Anything with an exotic name.

4   If you are playing a fruit machine and you lose all the change in your pocket, what do you do?

   a Stop before you lose any more.
   b Borrow a couple more coins from a friend, offering to split the take.
   c Change a big note in the hope of making a 'killing'.

5 Which holiday would you prefer?

  a A 'package' to a popular resort.
  b A mini cruise on a luxury liner.
  c Following the stars, overland to Katmandu.

6 What is your attitude to insurance schemes?

  a You would not sleep at night unless fully insured.
  b You never quite know what is insured and what is not.
  c You think insurance schemes are a waste of time.

7 What is your idea of a good driver? A person who:

  a Observes the speed limits meticulously.
  b Drives fairly fast but without loss of control.
  c Weaves through city traffic like a racing driver.

8 At a fun fair, which rides do you enjoy?

  a The carousel.
  b The water-splash.
  c The latest terror trip.

9 What do you think about smoking?

  a Too dangerous a habit to contemplate.
  b It doesn't bother you much one way or another.
  c A pleasurable 'kick' – and the health risk has been
    exaggerated.

10 When you play music at home what do you do?

  a Always keep the volume low so as not to disturb the
    neighbours.
  b Close the doors and windows if you want it loud.
  c Blast it out on powerful amplifiers.

11 You are asked to lay your hands on a guarantee form for
equipment you have bought. You could:

  a Find it immediately – you keep all documents in a safe place.
  b Probably find it if you rummage through a few obvious
    places.
  c You would not have a hope in hell – you probably threw it
    away with the wrapping.

12   Which of the following hobbies appeals to you most?

    a Stamp collecting.
    b Going to the theatre.
    c Sky diving.

13   In which city would you prefer to live?

    a Melbourne.
    b London.
    c New York.

14   If you go to a party, how do you like to dress?

    a Pretty and pleasant.
    b Colourful and sexy.
    c Flamboyant and outrageous.

15   If you won the pools, what would you do with the money?

    a Deposit it in a building society.
    b Play the Stock Exchange.
    c Put it all behind a make or break business venture.

16   How do you like people to think of you?

    a Good natured.
    b Witty and amusing.
    c Wild and unpredictable.

17   Your dream lover would be:

    a A good friend you have known for years.
    b A film star.
    c A Nobel prize winner you have never seen.

18   If you were working in an office and the fire alarm went off, what would you do?

    a Clear out on to the street immediately.
    b Sniff around the corridors to see what's up.
    c Carry on working – it's bound to be a false alarm or just a test.

19   Do you wear a safety belt if you are a passenger in a car?

    a Always, even in the back seat if there is a belt available.
    b Usually, especially in the front seat and on long journeys.
    c Seldom – you don't like that harnessed feeling.

20 You have the opportunity to spend a week in an exotic country that is currently troubled with political strife and terrorism. You would:

  a Decline the invitation.
  b Go, but stick around the hotel pool as much as possible.
  c Go and see everything there is to be seen despite the element of danger.

SCORING

Give yourself 2 points for each 'c' answer, and 1 point for each 'b' (all 'a's score zero).

Score: 0–9

You appear to be a very sensible and practical person, certainly not one to stick your neck out. While this is an admirable trait for the most part, is it not possible that you are sometimes over-cautious, bordering on the obsessional? Are you perhaps bored, and even a little boring? Would it not be fun, just occasionally, to break out of your somewhat mundane routine and do something just for the hell of it?

Score: 10–29

You appear to be a reasonably balanced kind of person, able to find a certain amount of fun and adventure without taking unnecessary risks. Stick with the happy medium.

Score: 30–40

Your lust for thrills seems a bit on the desperate side. You would probably benefit from controlling your impulses a bit more, and so, perhaps, would other people around you. Maybe you will settle down to a more level-headed existence when you get a bit older – if you live to be a bit older.

7

ARE YOU A HYPOCHONDRIAC?

Are you the kind of person who imagines illnesses? Do you worry unnecessarily about catching diseases? Are you racked by delusions that your body functions are failing? Everybody suffers ill health now and again and has a need to seek medical help, but a small minority of people seem compelled to invent symptoms where none exist – sometimes because of mistaken preconceptions, but more often as a sign of psychological stress or as a device for gaining attention and sympathy from other people. Answer the questions below to find out whether you are a normal person, sometimes healthy and sometimes sick, or a neurotic hypochondriac who inflates minor disturbances into catastrophic ailments.

1 Do you make a point of visiting your doctor whenever you are feeling 'out of sorts'?   *Yes   No*

2 Do you often suffer from poor appetite because of worry and anxiety?   *Yes   No*

3 Is your skin very sensitive and tender?   *Yes   No*

4 Do you frequently feel as if you are going to faint?   *Yes   No*

5 Would you say you have no more headaches than most people?   *Yes   No*

6 Do you sometimes feel a twitching of the face, head or shoulders?   *Yes   No*

7 Do you make a point of staying away from people who are sick in case you should catch whatever they've got?   *Yes   No*

8 On most mornings, do you wake up feeling well and strong?   *Yes   No*

9 Do you suffer a great deal from nervous exhaustion? *Yes No*

10 Do your friends and relatives consider you to be a sickly person? *Yes No*

11 Do you often feel a choking lump in your throat? *Yes No*

12 Do you take more than one type of pill in the course of an average week? *Yes No*

13 Do severe pains and aches make it impossible for you to concentrate on your work? *Yes No*

14 If your doctor told you he/she could find nothing wrong with you, would you have no difficulty in taking his or her word for it? *Yes No*

15 If you feel sick and feverish, would you expect to be right again after a good night's sleep? *Yes No*

16 Does back trouble run in your family? *Yes No*

17 Do other people often seem unsympathetic to you when you are feeling unwell? *Yes No*

18 Do you frequently suffer from constipation? *Yes No*

19 Do you think that vitamin tablets are a waste of time for anyone eating a reasonable diet? *Yes No*

20 Are you often bothered by palpitations of the heart? *Yes No*

21 Do you worry a lot about other members of your family getting ill? *Yes No*

22 Are you troubled by cold hands and feet even in warm weather? *Yes No*

23 Do you often have difficulty in breathing? *Yes No*

24 Would you say it is a waste of time going to the doctor with most mild complaints, such as coughs, headaches and stomach upsets? *Yes No*

25 Do you suffer a great deal from indigestion and stomach pains such that you think you may have ulcers? *Yes No*

26 Do you look at the colour of your tongue in the mirror
       most mornings?   *Yes*   *No*

27 Would you say you weigh yourself less than once a
       week on average?   *Yes*   *No*

28 Are you often troubled by noises in your ears?   *Yes*   *No*

29 Do you keep a medicine cabinet in your home that
       contains a great variety of leftovers from your previous
       prescriptions?   *Yes*   *No*

30 Do you have hot and cold spells for no apparent
       reason?   *Yes*   *No*

SCORING

Give yourself 1 point if you answered 'Yes' to questions 1, 2, 3, 4, 6, 7, 9, 10, 11, 12, 13, 16, 17, 18, 20, 21, 22, 23, 25, 26, 28, 29 and 30; and 1 point if you answered 'No' to questions 5, 8, 14, 15, 19, 24 and 27. This will give you a total score of between 0 and 30, which can be interpreted as follows:

Score: 0–5

You appear to be a very fortunate person who is seldom troubled by sickness, either real or imagined. Perhaps you are so healthy and happy that you find it difficult to sympathise with people who do suffer psychological and medical distress.

Score: 6–15

You are a fairly typical person – sometimes vulnerable to illness, particularly when you are run down physically or in low spirits psychologically. Medicine can sometimes help you; at other times it may be more important for you to learn how to relax, to restructure your lifestyle so that it is less stressful, and to be more optimistic, active and outgoing in your attitudes.

Score: 16—30

You appear to have an exaggerated concern with your health and body functions and would possibly qualify for the description of hypochondriacal.

While it is possible that you really are a genuinely sick person, the range of symptoms that you complain of makes this extremely unlikely. Of course, you may really be feeling pain and distress, and in this sense it is real, but you should investigate the possibility that most of it is of psychosomatic origin and could be more effectively treated by psychotherapy than by drugs and hospitals. Does your overconcern with health represent a kind of phobia (causing you to be ill as a result of self-fulfilling prophecy)? Or, do you feel stressed and unloved, such that you seek sympathetic attention from your doctor, family and friends? The nearer your score is to 30, the more important it is for you to admit the need for psychological rather than medical help.

8

HOW SHY ARE YOU?

A re you a shrinking violet or a brazen sunflower? Some people thrive on the company of others and come into their own in the midst of an audience. For others, meeting people is an excruciating experience, to be avoided if at all possible. Taking the initiative is something they would rather leave to someone else. Self-confidence is no certain measure of your worth as a person (some of the people most keen to present themselves publicly have the least reason to be proud of themselves). Nevertheless, you may be interested to find out how shy you are.

Answer the questions below as honestly as possible.

I   If you are meeting someone for the first time whom you are trying to impress, would you be:

    a Struck dumb and sweaty palmed?
    b Slightly flustered and overanxious to please?
    c Witty, lively and in command?

2   Do you feel most relaxed in the company of:

    a Just yourself and a good book?
    b One close friend?
    c A jovial crowd?

3   What would you do if you were having trouble finding a street address?

    a Try to work it out from the map.
    b Ask somebody of your own age and sex.
    c Accost the first intelligent looking person you see.

4   If you are going for a job interview, do you:

    a Speak very quietly and keep looking at the floor?
    b Attempt to hide your nerves by talking loudly?
    c Look the interviewer straight in the eye and speak clearly?

5 How would you best express your love for someone?

   a In a letter.
   b On the telephone.
   c In person – heart to heart.

6 How do you react to a compliment?

   a Blush, feel awkward, self-conscious, and lost for words.
   b Question their sincerity and deny that what they say is true.
   c Find a way of complimenting them in return.

7 When you are making conversation at a dinner party, do you feel the person you are talking to is:

   a Bored to tears by you?
   b Somewhat distracted?
   c Hanging on to your every word?

8 If a television crew was doing a street interview on a controversial news item, would you:

   a Avoid being asked by crossing the street?
   b Give an interview and kick yourself afterwards for not having said all the things you wanted to say?
   c Suavely and precisely express your opinion?

9 If you were in southern Europe and a friendly native pinched your bottom, would you:

   a Scurry away in terror?
   b Accept it as a quaint local custom?
   c Pinch their's back?

10 How do you relate to someone you meet in the lift?

   a Avoid all eye-contact?
   b Restrict yourself to innocuous comments about something like the weather?
   c Usually manage a joke or some kind of conversation?

11 You walk into a party and everyone seems to turn round and stare at you. Do you:

   a Burst into tears, assuming that something you are wearing is awful?
   b Whisper to your companion to indicate what the problem is?
   c Expect to turn heads wherever you go?

12   If you were asked to make a speech, would you:

    a Take a fistful of tranquillisers?
    b Keep it short?
    c Make it as interesting as possible to the listeners?

13   Someone with a very sexy voice gets you as a 'wrong number', do you:

    a Apologise for inconveniencing them?
    b Regret not keeping them on the phone?
    c Blatantly chat them up in an equally sexy voice?

14   If your boss was coming to dinner what would you wear?

    a Something discreet and quiet in a neutral colour.
    b Something that flattered you and brought out the colour of your eyes.
    c A rather provocative little number with a low neckline.

15   If somebody uses bad language in your company, how do you react?

    a It makes you feel really upset and flustered.
    b You ignore them, thinking them rude and inadequate.
    c You are quite capable of reciprocating if it's directed at you.

16   If you saw two people you know in a 'punch up' would you:

    a Feel your heart in your mouth?
    b Decide not to interfere if it did not concern you?
    c Go over and try to persuade them to break it up?

17   What do you think of topless beaches?

    a They are embarrassing and shameless.
    b OK if you've got a good figure.
    c The only way to sunbathe.

18   What do you think is the most becoming skirt length?

    a Full length.
    b Below the knee.
    c The mini.

19   If you felt you were entitled to a raise in pay, how would you behave?

    a Hope that the boss would eventually realise your worth – you couldn't possibly say anything.

b Find an opportunity to slip in a hint about having been with the firm for a long time and always being short of money.

c Make a specific appointment to state your claim directly, with written details in support.

20 If a crisis arose in your personal life, who would you feel able to tell?

a Nobody – you'd keep it to yourself.

b You would phone up a counselling service.

c You would confide in a close friend or relative.

SCORING

Give yourself 2 points for each 'a' answer, one point for each 'b' and zero for each 'c'. Add up your total score and interpret it as follows:

Score: 0–10

You are certainly 'not backward in coming forward', as the saying goes. Self-imposed social isolation will never be a problem with you. However, it is possible that your self-confidence sometimes tends towards impertinence, arrogance, or interference which could grate on others. Generally speaking, your brand of bubbling extraversion is a happy condition, and you should get on very well in the world. Just remember that a degree of modesty and sensitivity to the needs of others is necessary if the life and soul of the party is not to descend into a crashing bore.

Score: 11–29

Yours is the typical human condition, sometimes quite pushy and outgoing, and sometimes reticent and retiring. You probably think you would be better off bolder than you are, but the betting is you are more aware of your shy streak than are other people, who frequently admire your pluck. And even if you are a little coy and self-conscious at times, that is no bad thing – probably it is a great deal more attractive to other people than you realise.

Score: 30–40

You appear to have an excessive fear of other people evaluating you lowly. So what, they cannot bite. Does it really matter all that much what they think about you? Is it not possible they are too concerned about how they are coming across to you to notice any social deficiency on your part? For all their bravado, the betting is they are inwardly just as shy as you. Try to get outside of yourself by thinking more about the other people you meet – what their problems might be and how they are feeling. To think only about the impression you are making is a form of self-indulgence.

9

WHAT MAKES YOU LAUGH?

Most people pride themselves in having a good sense of humour. But what exactly do they mean by that? Do they mean they have a *broad* sense of humour and will laugh at almost anything: or do they mean they are very *discriminating* in what they regard as funny? The fact is that, where jokes are concerned, 'one man's meat is another man's poison', and the most useful assessment of people's sense of humour is one that puts them into laughter categories.

Find out what is your preferred brand of humour by answering these questions:

1 Which of the following films would you see by preference?
   a A 'Carry On' film.
   b 'Animal House', or one of the other American campus-life films.
   c A Monty Python film.
   d A Marx Brothers film.

2 Buying a friend a birthday card, you choose:
   a A card with a peep-hole on the front, resembling a 'derriere' which turns out to be part of a cake inside.
   b A card which says, 'I was going to send you a birthday cake with candles, but the fire brigade wasn't available to stand by'.
   c A witty innuendo, such as 'I can't give you a present, but I can give you a past'.
   d A picture of a man icing a tuna fish with the message, 'I-cing a tuna for you on your birthday'.

3 A group of people in the pub are telling risqué jokes that get dirtier as the beer flows. You:
   a Laugh louder than most and match them with filthy tales of your own.

b Tell scandalous stories concerning the misdeeds and
misfortunes of people you all know.

c Find it slightly distasteful and seek to elevate the
conversation to a higher level.

d Try to deflect them with a few 'knock-knock' jokes.

4   You are giving a child a humorous book. You would buy:

a Billy Bunter.

b Tom and Jerry.

c Asterix the Gaul.

d Enid Blyton.

5   If you went into a joke shop, what would you buy?

a A whoopee cushion.

b Stink bombs and itching powder.

c A phoney brandy glass.

d A false nose, moustache and glasses.

6   Which of these comedians do you like most?

a Benny Hill.

b Bob Hope.

c Woody Allen.

d Spike Milligan.

7   What do you think of practical jokes?

a You like to see people embarrassed, that is, caught 'with
their trousers down'.

b They're terrific – you love seeing other people 'cut down to
size'.

c OK, so long as they are good fun and have an element of wit
and originality.

d You like pranks best when they are silly and harmless.

8   In which situation are you most likely to clown around? When
you:

a Relax with a bunch of work-mates in the pub or at a party.

b See a chance to get a rise out of somebody pompous or over-
serious.

c Are with somebody you can spar with on equal terms.

d Get an uncontrollable fit of the giggles.

9 Although graffiti is defacing, it is often amusing. Which of
these examples amuses you most?

a Notice on a toilet wall: 'Beware low Limbo dancers'.

b On a theatre wall: 'Danny La Rue is a real drag'.

c On the wall of the British Museum: 'Give Elgin back his
marbles'.

d On a conductor's podium: 'Gone Chopin. Bach in a minuet'.

10 Which of the following jokes makes you laugh most?

a Two men in a urinal – one suddenly turns (mid-stream) to
the other and says, 'Hey, aren't you Frank Sinatra?'

b Pompous woman: 'What an ugly portrait.' Art dealer: 'That
madam, is a mirror.'

c The Irishman who is granted three wishes by a genie, asks
for an inexhaustible bottle of Guinness, then uses up the
other two wishes for two more of the same.

d Why does a giraffe have a long neck? Because it's feet smell!

11 What slogan might you wear on a t-shirt?

a Easy but not cheap.

b Have a nice day (before some bastard louses it up).

c Make love not war (I'm married, I do both).

d E.T. phone home.

SCORING

Mostly 'a's

You are an earthy person with a straightforward, basic approach to
what makes you laugh. You are seldom offended by jokes that others
find vulgar or crude. In fact, you derive considerable enjoyment from
them. Good for you, but don't forget, 'there's a time and a place'.

Mostly 'b's

The banana peel joke might have been invented for you. Here, and
probably also in other areas of life, you have an aggressive, competitive streak and enjoy the game of one-upmanship. If you are not
already at the top, you are no doubt striving hard to improve your
position in the pecking order. Take care not to expose your hostility too
blatantly.

Mostly 'c's

Your sense of humour is tuned more towards sophisticated, intellectual types of jokes. You appreciate the off-beat wit and satire of many fringe comedians, and possibly pride yourself in a scintillating personal line of repartee. Very commendable, but take care you do not become a 'humour snob', unable to enjoy a good belly laugh at down-to-earth events.

Mostly 'd's

You respond best to inoffensive jokes, loving a good giggle at playful nonsense, innocuous puns, incongruities and *non-sequiturs*. Some people might think of you as childish and immature in this taste, but your sense of humour does not hurt anyone, and who wants to grow old anyway?

10

YOUR CORE VALUES: CAREER,

FAMILY OR ROMANCE?

To a large extent, people are motivated by values – what they think are important goals and aspects of life. These are notoriously different from one person to another. We cannot assume that just because we personally are obsessed by religion, or sport, or travel, or sex, that everyone else in the world is similarly inclined. It is only by understanding the values that underlie and guide people's behaviour that we can really know what makes them 'tick'.

Values refer to choices or priorities. Everybody pays lip service to freedom and equality – these are two values that are almost universally rated as desirable. But suppose you have to choose between them, to decide which is more important? In this circumstance, right-wingers usually prefer freedom, while left-wingers choose equality. Some things, such as adult movies and motor cycling, are positive values to some individuals and negative to others but, generally speaking, values can only be assessed in relative terms.

Three major aspects of life which are likely to fall into some degree of conflict, with the result that priorities become important, are career, family and romance. This is particularly true for women. Some obvious instances come to mind: a woman who wants to have children is bound to consider what effect this will have on her career. In their early years especially, children require a great deal of attention and affection, and whatever their intentions before their children are born, most women find it difficult to leave them for a working day and hard to concentrate on any creative work in their presence. This dilemma occurs more and more these days as a higher proportion of women seek to combine motherhood with career development. Likewise, the person who devotes him or herself entirely to professional achievement is likely to neglect his/her partner. There is insufficient time for weekends in the country, romantic gestures, such as buying flowers or walking together in the park.

It is easy to see why each of these aspects of life can become so important that people become single-minded in pursuit of them. A career is a pathway to wealth and fame, and often also a means for making oneself desirable to the opposite sex. However, like almost any activity that requires investment of time and energy, whether it be jogging, cleaning the house or dieting, the pursuit of a career can easily become an end in itself, so that the individual becomes a workaholic with no time for, or interest in, anything else.

A career is also a source of identity – a means by which people know 'who they are'. 'What do you do?', is one of the first questions asked of us on meeting someone new at a party. And if people are asked to describe themselves, they usually give their occupation shortly after their sex and physical characteristics. Pride in our job is therefore a major basis of self-esteem.

The importance of the family is in the sense of purpose that it brings to our lives. While many people with family ties consciously resent their obligations and commitments and wish they were free to travel, meet new people and pursue their pleasures, this view of 'greener grass' is generally illusory. Research suggests that people are more stable and happy in the long term if they have clear social roles to perform and others who are dependent on them.

The rewards of romance are equally obvious. People who are in love are happy in a much more positive, euphoric sense. There is some evidence that the chemical state of the brain of a person in love is similar to the 'high' produced by drugs such as amphetamine. Since these drugs are addictive, this might explain the withdrawal symptoms observed following a broken love affair, and since they are similar to chemicals found in chocolate, this might explain why many people binge on chocolate when they are feeling unloved. Being in love is a 'peak experience', which is great at the time, but difficult to sustain over a period of time.

Clearly, each of the three prime values – career, family and romance – have rewards to offer. Which we focus our life upon depends upon our constitutional temperament, for example, whether we prefer stability or excitement, ever-changing social contacts or a few special friends, as well as early experiences of success and failure in various enterprises which have brought us to our present condition. To find out what motivates you particularly, answer the questions below.

I   The greatest compliment anyone could pay you would be to say:

a What a great job you make of bringing up your family.
b That you deserve to be at the top of your chosen career/profession.
c How happy and contented your lover looks since they met you.

2 At Christmas, it is important for you to:

a Have a traditional family celebration.
b Send presents to essential business contacts.
c Be exclusively with your partner.

3 You have to give up your job to look after your children. You feel:

a It is the right and proper way to proceed.
b Frustrated that you will not be able to fulfil your ambitions.
c Relieved when they go to school so you have more time to spend with your partner.

4 Where do you want to live?

a In the country, where there is fresh air and things can grow.
b In a big city, where you can be at the heart of a thriving business community.
c By the sea with stunning sunsets to share with your soul-mate.

5 You dress mostly in clothes that are:

a Comfortable and practical for wearing around the house.
b Smart and creating an impression of elegant efficiency.
c Alluring and attractive to the opposite sex.

6 You prefer to eat:

a A well-cooked meal at home.
b In an expensive, chic restaurant.
c In a candlelit French bistro.

7 Your energy is well spent on:

a Keeping your home spotless.
b Talking at length to colleagues to keep your finger on the pulse at work.
c Strenuous exercise to keep your figure in shape.

8   A person who is power and money motivated is:

    a Missing out on the real rewards of family life.
    b A real go-getter deserving of admiration.
    c Losing touch with the joy of romance.

9   Someone who is prepared to devote themselves to finding an ideal mate is:

    a Chasing rainbows.
    b A romantic fool.
    c An idealist.

10   A secure and happy home and family life is:

    a All you could ever desire.
    b Not enough to satisfy you.
    c The way you like to think of your parents.

11   Most of your friends are:

    a Other parents.
    b People connected with work.
    c Other young couples.

12   You choose as a partner:

    a Someone you can trust to be a good parent.
    b An independent person with his/her own career.
    c Someone you are madly in love with.

13   The pictures in your photograph album are of:

    a Several generations of family and friends.
    b Various achievements in your life, for example, winning prizes at school or university.
    c Yourself and your lover on holiday in various places.

14   The politician who would get your vote would be lobbying for:

    a Better education.
    b Cuts in income tax.
    c More support for the arts.

15   On what does most of your food budget go?

    a Meals for the family.
    b Expense account lunches.
    c Banquets for your lover.

16 When you are feeling emotional or upset, the cause more often than not is:

   a Problems at home.
   b Trouble at work.
   c Conflict with your partner.

17 To whom do you relate most comfortably?

   a Relatives.
   b Business colleagues.
   c Your boy/girlfriend.

18 Your daydreams take the form of:

   a Decorating your dream home.
   b Being eminently successful in your chosen career.
   c Going on a romantic voyage with your lover.

19 A woman whose lifestyle you admire is:

   a Queen Elizabeth.
   b Lady Thatcher.
   c The Duchess of York.

20 You feel in your element when you are:

   a On home territory, surrounded by your loved ones.
   b In an office equipped with the latest technology.
   c Anywhere with your lover by your side to provide strength and support.

21 A gift you would really appreciate right now would be:

   a A new vacuum cleaner.
   b Next year's diary.
   c A recording of your favourite love song.

22 What aspect of shopping do you find irritating?

   a Being patronised because you are a mere housewife/ husband.
   b Time wasted standing in queues.
   c Drabness in shops and lack of glamour generally.

23 You share a sense of humour with:

   a Members of your family.
   b Mates at work.
   c Your partner.

24   Birthdays can be pretty expensive when:

    a Youngsters in the family circle are growing up.
    b There is a continuous stream of them at work.
    c You want to spend all your money on a fabulous gift for your lover.

25   One of the most important decisions you have made recently was:

    a Choosing a new house.
    b Making up your mind on what career to follow.
    c Deciding on getting married.

26   A friend suggests you emigrate and join them in a far-off country. That would depend upon whether:

    a You could bear to leave some of your relatives behind.
    b Your career would be advanced by going.
    c Your partner would go with you.

27   You can't imagine how people survive without:

    a The solid support of a family.
    b A decent job with prospects.
    c Someone to be in love with.

28   From quite an early age, you regarded life as pretty futile without:

    a Making a good marriage.
    b Recognition of your talents.
    c A generous helping of romance.

29   You read books about:

    a Family units and the events which affect their lives.
    b Adventure and exploration.
    c Love and romance.

30   Children should be brought up to believe in:

    a Making a stable relationship as a base for building a family.
    b Making the most of their talents and ability.
    c Seeking out happiness and beauty.

31   An elderly relative gets sick. You would:

    a Personally nurse them back to health.

b Get them the best possible nursing you could afford.
c Feel profoundly sad and cry often.

32 You feel tremendous sympathy for:

a Single-parent families.
b People who have been made redundant.
c People who suffer a broken engagement.

33 People whose homes are always in a mess are:

a Lazy and undisciplined.
b Too busy with more important things.
c Charmingly Bohemian (unconventional).

34 In the luggage department of a store you would buy:

a A roomy shopping trolley or large picnic basket.
b A dress/suit bag or executive briefcase.
c A good quality overnight bag or a snazzy wallet.

35 The cosmetics and toiletries you use are primarily:

a To keep your skin clean and fresh smelling.
b To preserve a well-groomed and sophisticated image.
c To make yourself alluring and fatal to the opposite sex.

36 In a competition, you win the star prize of two weeks for two on a Caribbean island. You:

a Give the tickets as a honeymoon present to a couple in your family who are getting married.
b Ensure your promotion by offering them to your boss.
c Take off with your sweetheart.

37 Having strong religious beliefs is:

a An essential part of living.
b Somewhat outmoded and outdated.
c A means to ritual splendour and passion.

38 Knowledge is worthless without:

a Good common sense to back it up.
b Long-term experience and expertise.
c A lively imagination.

39 When the phone rings at home, it is usually about:

a Family matters.

    b A business call.

    c Your lover missing you.

40 If you are forced, by financial circumstance, to work, what do you do?

    a Choose something you can do at home, so as not to interfere with your family life.

    b You would never be forced since you are already strongly motivated to work.

    c Opt to do something that is artistic and creative.

SCORING

Add up the number of 'a', 'b' and 'c' answers you gave, to provide you with three scores, each in the range of 0–40.

Mostly 'a's

Your major concern is with the *family*. Probably you have children of your own or are planning to start a family fairly soon. If not, then you are the kind of person who values the parental home, gravitates there often, and keeps in touch with brothers, sisters and other relatives. You are the kind of person who would not want to be away from home at Christmas.

If you are a woman, you would be described as 'traditional'; if a man, you would be seen as a devoted husband, father or son, who spends as much time as possible with his family. None of this is anything to be ashamed of.

Close involvement with the family brings the rewards of stability, continuity and identity – a sense of long-term purpose. The chances are that you keep a photograph album full of pictures of family events, such as holidays, birthdays, Christmas and weddings, which help you to keep track of where you have come from, and help you to know who you are. You understand your roles and duties and your estimation of yourself is greatly enhanced by the knowledge that other people need you.

It is easy to lose sight of these virtues when we read about the violence that takes place within families and today's high divorce rates, and hear people moan about lack of freedom and the high cost of children's clothing and schooling. All these negative aspects are real, but families also provide many rewards and satisfactions that are too often taken for granted. If the family was all bad news (as some radical psychiatrists have suggested) there would be no need to feel sorry for orphans. But the truth is we do, and for good reason; the family is the main source of 'base-camp' security and self-esteem.

Mostly 'b's

The core of your value system focuses on your *career* ambitions. Probably you had some early success and encouragement at school and have some talents and abilities that you feel should not go to waste. You may have embarked upon a career and climbed several rungs of the ladder already. If so, this is likely to be within an occupation that is intrinsically interesting and creative and in which you can see prospects for future progress and achievement. For example, actors, artists, scientists and business people are more likely to devote themselves wholeheartedly to a career than typists or assembly workers. Jobs in the latter categories are more often viewed as premarriage stop-gaps or unpleasant necessities.

People who make successful careers are not only talented and achievement-oriented, they are also usually extravert and socially skilled as well. It is difficult to make progress in the business world, or any other field, without meeting people and exercising some degree of diplomacy. Whether one is dealing with bosses or assistants, rivals, clients or the public at large, some capacity to 'win friends and influence people' is usually a prerequisite. Warmth and tact are partly innate traits, although some of the fundamental rules can be taught and applied consciously.

The rewards of high level career achievement are obvious. *Power, wealth and fame* are satisfying in their own right, and carry much spin-off, such as the opportunity to travel, dress well, eat in good restaurants, meet interesting people, and be attractive to the opposite sex. After all, 'Power is a great aphrodisiac'.

Critics of the lifestyle say that the rat race leads to the neglect of friends and more important values, and that if family and romance are sacrificed too much, a degree of emptiness is ultimately experienced.

Mostly 'c's

You are the type of person who lives primarily for *love and romance*. Perhaps you are in love at this moment, and seeing the world through the proverbial rose-coloured spectacles. Some say this is an illusion, but others make an equal case that it is the greatest reality. Who can say which is more true?

Perhaps you have recently emerged from an intense love affair that gave life a new meaning, and this you are seeking to reconstruct. Or you have been there many times before and know that life is most exciting and exhilarating when you are in love.

Even if you are not in love with a particular partner, and never have been in the past, you may be in love with the idea of love and create it out of your own imagination. You are probably an avid reader of romantic fiction who harks back to days of medieval chivalry or Victorian dignity and elegance. You prefer to focus upon the beautiful things in life and ignore the pain, practicalities and dross.

Whatever your situation, you may count yourself fortunate, for it takes benevolence and a feeling of well-being to love. The chances are you are still young, for a romantic view of the world is notoriously difficult to sustain with age. On the other hand, the belief that 'love makes the world go round' is not just the temporary preserve of youth.

Which is best?

It is not our intention to judge which of these three life philosophies is the most satisfying or virtuous. People are different and must follow the dictates of their heart in such matters. Each orientation has its particular rewards and draw-backs. Hopefully, what this quiz has achieved is to bring you to a more explicit understanding of what motivates you in life and where your true values lie.

II

ARE YOU BOUND FOR SUCCESS?

How often have you asked yourself, 'What have they got that I haven't got?' Why has that person succeeded in life when you have not, when he/she does not appear to be any more talented or intelligent than yourself? Is there somebody you grew up with and did just as well as at school who has built a brilliant career while you remain in the occupational doldrums? Does somebody else always land the lead part in your local operatic or drama society when you are convinced you could do it equally well? Are your friends more organised in their love lives than you despite the fact that you are every bit as attractive and eligible? Successful people share certain qualities that enable them to rise a notch or two above the ordinary mortals about them.

MOTIVATION

The first outstanding quality of successful people is their drive and determination. Many people sit around on their ample posteriors wondering why it is not happening for them, without ever realising that the vast majority of successful people are more than just lucky – they nearly always have had to put in a great deal of hard work.

Reading the biographies of famous people is revealing: most of them are in the habit of waking at a very early hour or working late into the night, and setting aside specific hours of the day in which they work. This is true of the top writers, artists, scientists, politicians, business executives and sports stars. Some work better in the morning and others in the evening, but almost invariably they have put long hours into their chosen occupation. Obviously, it is impossible to become a world-champion boxer or swimmer without hard training, but much the same applies to other fields of endeavour.

This implies strong commitment to a chosen field. It is no good being highly ambitious and energetic in general – some degree of *focus* is necessary. You have to know (or decide) as precisely as possible in what line you wish to reach the top. Otherwise, you become a 'Jack of all trades and master of none'.

Having decided on the field, a great deal of *persistence* is necessary. This means sticking at a project night and day until it is completed. Many people fail in life because they abandon their plans as soon as the going gets rough. At the first hint of difficulty or disappointment, they give up what they were trying to achieve, and either do nothing at all, or switch to another venture, in which the same sequence tends to happen. Success only comes by staying with a particular assignment and seeing it through.

Consider Richard Wagner's major artistic achievement, *The Ring of the Nibelung*. From the time he began researching Norse mythology in order to write the story, to the completion of the musical score, it took him 34 years to write. For most of this time he could see no prospect of it ever being publicly performed because he felt that it could only be mounted in a theatre specially constructed for it, which he would also have to design and build himself. This required a great deal of faith and funding which was not available at the time and which might never have been forthcoming. It is almost impossible to imagine what devotion Wagner must have had to this project in order to see it through against such odds.

True motivation comes from *within*. External forms of reward (incentives and inducements) are generally much less effective as regards increasing productivity and creativity than is intrinsic interest, while punishments and threats are more often than not counterproductive. People generally work less effectively when bullied and harassed than when they are left to get on with things at their own pace.

The distinction between intrinsic and extrinsic motivation is nicely illustrated in a story told by an eminent psychologist concerning the behaviour of his son. Apparently, the boy used to enjoy tidying his bedroom every morning until one day his father made the mistake of rewarding him with money for his efforts. The result was that the boy thereafter refused to tidy his bedroom without an advance guarantee of payment, and what is more, he no longer took pleasure in doing so – he now viewed it as drudgery. The key to success in any field is to love what you are doing for its own sake. Not everybody is fortunate enough to be able to work at a job they really enjoy, but those who are wedded to their work in this sense are the ones that tend to get on in it.

Lack of persistence is one reason why women have difficulty competing with men in so many occupations. Experiments by social psychologists show that mastery is a more powerful motive in boys, whereas affiliation is more important to girls. A typical experiment involves giving an insoluble problem to teenage boys and girls and observing how long they persist in trying to solve it. In the absence of any social contact, boys typically work at it for longer than girls. However, if the experimenter is alongside giving them encouragement, girls persist just as long as boys – apparently because they are keen to please the experimenter. As a broad generalisation, women try to build relationships, while men try to get things done. Of course, there are many other differences between men and women that are important to occupational success, as well as a great deal of social and personal prejudice operating against women, but motivational differences are among the most important.

CHARISMA

Certain personality attributes also make for success in life, and these are summarised in the buzz-word, charisma. Literally, charisma means charm or magic, but this does not mean that it is beyond analysis. To some extent charisma, like beauty, is in the eye of the beholder – it is attributed to us by other people. What they believe about our personality, talents, power and social position determines what they see in us. The person who is introduced as 'president of the society', 'star of the show' or 'Pulitzer prize winner' starts off with a tremendous advantage and usually strikes us as impressive, regardless of their behaviour or utterances.

The Peter Sellers film, *Being There* was a very funny illustration of imputed charisma. A gardener, mis-identified as a guru called Chancey Gardner, rises to great social and political heights on the basis of monosyllabic statements about flowers and plants that are interpreted by his audience as metaphorical comments upon the state of the nation and the world. Andy Warhol was, in some people's opinion, a real-life equivalent in the field of visual arts.

But part of charisma also derives from the personal qualities of the individual. *Warmth* is a very important characteristic, and this amounts to the ability to make people around us feel important and good. The secret is to find things about other people that you can genuinely admire and comment about, while ignoring their less desirable traits. By smiling and saying positive things, we make ourselves attractive to other people, and because they find our company rewarding they are more inclined to put opportunities our way.

Some people are selectively nice only to others whom they think are influential or potentially useful, while presenting their usual miserable selves to everyone else. The trouble is that they make bad miscalculations as to who is important and who is not. In addition, their behaviour is usually transparent to those they are seeking to impress, with the result that it is dismissed as superficial contrivance. True warmth, which comes from the heart and does not discriminate among targets in this way, is easily recognised.

Another important component of charisma is *confidence*. People who get on in the world exude an aura of being in control of the situation and at peace with themselves. They show a high level of self-esteem and give the impression that they are happy with their looks, dress, behaviour and progress in life. They show few signs of nervousness or desperation such as fidgetting, stammering, smoking and temper outbursts. To use a popular colloquialism, they appear as 'together' individuals.

Although charisma comes out of high self-esteem and social status, it is not helped by unsubtle boasting. Successful people do not go round telling other people how beautiful and brilliant they are and that they drive a Porsche. These things are only impressive if they are discovered indirectly by other people. The individual who finds it necessary to trumpet his/her wealth or virtue betrays an inner sense of insecurity concerning his/her self-worth.

The third major trait that is commonly found in people we think of as charismatic is *expressiveness*. Successful people are usually able to give of themselves rather freely in social and public situations. They are good at communicating their thoughts and feelings by what they say (whether in formal speeches or casual conversations) and by various non-verbal means (that we call body language). They are likely to be expressive in artistic media such as painting, music and theatrical performance, and they are good at role-playing (the everyday application of acting skill). Film stars and TV personalities nearly always have this kind of charisma, but so do many people who are successful in other fields, such as business and politics.

It is not easy to acquire charisma when it is not there naturally, and there is mutual interplay between success and charisma (each feeding the other), but any kind of activity that builds confidence and self-esteem is helpful. This may include taking elocution lessons, buying some good-quality, fashionable clothes, or attending evening classes to expand one's education. Some initial outlay and effort may be necessary, but the rewards are cumulative and may be considerable.

OPENNESS TO EXPERIENCE

People who are successful in life usually have a great lust for life. They are curious and exploratory – perhaps even sensation-seeking. They travel widely and like to keep up with what is going on in the world by reading quality newspapers, watching TV news and documentaries and going to see avante-garde films and plays. In these and other respects, they are opposite to the rather staid and conventional person who likes to stay home and avoid novel experiences.

The probable reason for this link is that success often depends upon being innovative and grasping an opportunity at the brief moment that it presents itself – and this may entail taking chances. Successful people, therefore, often have something of the gambler in them. In fact, they may succeed only after many of their other enterprises have failed. The person who is so afraid of failure that he/she never makes a move without thinking it through very carefully is likely to end up missing the boat. Thus conservatism is not conducive to outstanding success in life; a certain amount of flexibility and willingness to experiment is more beneficial.

RESILIENCE

The ability to 'bounce back' after misfortune or failure is a quality that most successful people also display. People who collapse completely after a set-back and who lapse into a long-term depression are not likely to get on in the world.

Many great authors had difficulty in getting their books published. Agatha Christie was rejected by seventeen publishing companies before her first thriller was accepted and Dr Seuss, whom many regard as the outstanding children's author of modern times, also suffered many rejections from publishers before one finally recognised his genius. Guiseppe Verdi, the most celebrated Italian composer of all time, was turned down by the Milan Conservatoire of Music on grounds of insufficient talent, and many film stars, such as Harrison Ford, can describe the frustration of being rejected for bit parts before they hit the big time.

Success often depends upon having faith in yourself and what you have to offer the world. This should not take the form of boastful arrogance (which combined with experience of failure may lead to something approximating to paranoia), but having a quiet confidence and willingness to carry on presenting your talents, ideas and work.

A popular cop-out is to convince yourself that social rewards are restricted to in-groups of people who scratch each other's back – conspiracies of Masons, Jews, homosexuals, the Mafia, Oxbridge graduates or such-like. By hard work and perseverance it is possible to overcome social barriers. Some people even capitalise on their disadvantages. Charles Dickens wrote brilliantly of the experiences of his deprived childhood and Charlie Chaplin made his mark expressing the viewpoint of a little tramp – not far removed from what might have seemed his natural destination. Woody Allen achieved fame by representing the plight of the sexually unattractive male (the creep), and Salvador Dali turned borderline schizophrenia into creative genius. Many great writers and artists feed off their personal tragedies rather than allow themselves to be consumed with anger and self-pity.

SELF-ACTUALISATION

Clearly, a great many attributes go to make up what might be called creativity or the optimal personality. The most famous study of this question is that of the American humanistic psychologist, Abraham Maslow, who in his book *Motivation and Personality* (1970), described the characteristics of what he called 'self-actualising' adults. Maslow believed that psychology spent too much time studying neurotic and maladapted people, and that what was needed by way of antidote was a study of people who were fully-functioning, happy and successful.

Among the characteristics that Maslow found to be typical of self-actualisers were the following: 'an efficient perception of reality and comfortable relations with it', acceptance (of self, others and nature), spontaneity, problem-centring, a need for privacy, autonomy, continued freshness of appreciation, 'peak experiences' (the capacity to enjoy moments of ecstacy), deep and profound relationships with a small number of select people, 'democratic' character structure (lack of authoritarianism), a non-hostile sense of humour, clear discrimination between means and ends, creativity, and a transcendence of the particular culture. This picture is consistent with what has been said above about the attributes that make for success in almost any walk of life.

SPECIAL PROBLEMS OF WOMEN

Although we have said that social barriers should not be called upon as an excuse for not succeeding in life, there is no doubt that when women are trying to compete in traditionally male occupations, they often face special difficulties and decisions. Various strategies may be adopted (consciously or unconsciously) in such circumstances:

A woman may take a tough, masculine or 'butch' attitude in the belief that it is necessary to imitate men in order to compete with them. For example, she may emulate their appearance, wearing tailored suits and shirts and cutting her hair short. She may drink double whiskies or pints of bitter and tell vulgar jokes in the pub. She may make frequent attempts to shatter the egos of her competitors and speak sharply to secretaries and assistants.

A second approach is the exact opposite – that of exploiting the traditional feminine charms and wiles. For example, provocative and alluring clothes may be worn to the office (plunging necklines, split skirts and the like), helpless tears and pleading may be used to gain an advantage, and flirtatious gestures used to disarm the managing director, headmaster, producer (or whomever).

Thirdly some women (and men too) adopt a social climbing strategy, believing that success is best gained by associations and fabrications (a trait that is commonly referred to as 'snobbery'). Such women contrive to wear fashionable and expensive-looking clothes and jewellery, invoke influential social contacts whenever there is a problem to be solved, and their first priority in difficult times is to maintain status symbols, demarcations and the trappings of success. They may arrive deliberately late in order to effect a grand entrance and their social diary takes precedence over output in line with the belief that it is who you know that really counts.

Each of these strategies has been known to work for some women some of the time, but there is a distinct danger of backfire with all three (people are not always as gullible as they appear). The most reliable path to success for a woman in most fields of endeavour is to be found in genuine talent and performance, not in postures and deceptions. The best advice is to forget about the fact that you are female and concentrate on just doing the job well.

ARE YOU IN THE RIGHT JOB?

Some of the personality quizzes in this book bear on your prospects of success in life. For example, it helps to be tactful, imaginative, something of a risk-taker (though not totally reckless) and not too shy or stress-susceptible (hypochondriac). Your core values will define the field in which you seek success and, not surprisingly, the career orientation is the one that best predicts motivation to achieve in business, art or science. But occupational success also depends importantly on not getting into a rut with one's job. Advancement depends upon contentment and enthusiasm, rather than boredom and stress. That is why the quiz below has been devised to identify 'square pegs'.

I   What do Monday mornings mean to you?

  a The Monday Blues – a wave of depression seems to sweep over you.

  b They're great – first day to get stuck in to an exciting new week.

  c Mornings never were your best time – you warm up around 6 pm.

2   Are you particular about the way you dress for work?

  a It would not matter a damn what you wore, nobody important ever sees you.

  b Most of the time you try to make an effort to look presentable.

  c You go to great pains to co-ordinate your wardrobe and dress appropriately to suit the occasion.

3   How do you get on with your workmates?

  a Fine – there is a really friendly and supportive work atmosphere.

  b You sometimes have little tiffs and feel threatened by the competition.

  c You are totally fed up with all the bitching and backbiting that goes on.

4   When your boss is out of town, which of the following would you do?

    a Put your feet up and call your friends long distance.

    b Get on with the project in hand – the boss's presence makes no difference to your output.

    c Ease up and take a longer than usual lunch hour.

5 Does your favourite hobby encroach on your work time?

    a Your hobby is the most important aspect of your life and you find it saps more and more of your energy at home and work.

    b You try to keep business and pleasure separate.

    c You enjoy your job as much as any hobby.

6 What is your attitude to having a family?

    a You love children and can easily mix family life with your career.

    b You would prefer to stay home and bring up children.

    c Having children would interfere with your career plans.

7 If you are at a party and someone asks you what you do, how do you respond?

    a Try to change the subject – you are so ashamed of your job.

    b Give them a brief company profile.

    c State your occupation and leave it at that.

8 If there was a flu epidemic that kept the majority of staff off sick, what would you do?

    a Cope as well as you could, helping out in all departments until the work force was back to full strength.

    b Pretend you had caught the bug and stay home too.

    c Agree to work late if you are paid overtime.

9 What would be your first reaction to a summons by the boss?

    a Panic – you rush to the cloakroom (wash room) and freshen up.

    b Guilt in case they have discovered something stupid you have done.

    c Pleasure at the opportunity to discuss your latest project.

10 How often do nausea and tense headaches mar your working day?

    a When you have an important appointment/presentation you have not prepared for sufficiently.

b Almost constantly.

c You are so involved in your work you haven't time for such indulgences.

11 If you had to work over the weekend because of a special event, how would you feel?

a Furious to be forced to give up your free time.

b You'd tell your boss you intend making up the time due to you by taking an extended holiday.

c Offer your full support, realising that clock-watching does not make for success in business.

12 Do you approve of office romance? **?**

a Why else would you bother working for this company?

b You would not actively encourage or discourage it.

c You are content with your current relationship and would prefer not to complicate your work life.

13 What course of action would you take if night-time study could improve your position at work?

a Temporarily abandon your social life and get busy.

b Have a go at doing the course without letting it interfere with your social life.

c Think to yourself 'so what', you'll probably change jobs soon anyway.

14 What would you do if a rival company offered you a slightly higher salary to join it?

a Politely decline because you are happy in your present job.

b Suggest to your boss that you might leave unless he/she matches the offer.

c Accept the offer without hesitation.

15 What are your chances of promotion? Are you likely to get a step up the ladder in:

a 6 months?

b 2 years?

c When your boss retires?

16 When you have a business appointment how punctual are you?

a You are meticulous about timekeeping.

b You try not to keep people waiting, but are sometimes so busy it's unavoidable.

c People don't bother to be on time to meet you since you are notoriously late.

17 How would you react to a phone ringing in an adjacent empty office?

a Answer the call and take a helpful message.

b Say the party is out and hang up.

c Leave it to ring, you've got your own problems.

18 Do you enjoy social contact with your workmates after office hours?

a Yes, they're a great team and you share a lot of interests.

b You occasionally meet for a drink after work or invite them home.

c When you shut that office door at 5.30 pm, you just want to forget the lot of them.

19 Do you think the company you work for should acquire all the latest technology?

a New fangled gadgets will always be a mystery to you. You can't be bothered retraining yourself to use them.

b Yes, progress can only be achieved by employing the most advanced equipment.

c It makes you a bit fed up when you have just got used to the machines you already use.

20 Do you find it easy to concentrate on your work?

a No difficulty, your job is so absorbing.

b You sometimes find yourself daydreaming.

c You never pay much attention to what you're doing – it's all on automatic pilot.

SCORING

Give yourself points as follows in answer to the questions:

1	a 3	b 1	c 2			11	a 3	b 2	c 1		
2	a 3	b 2	c 1			12	a 3	b 2	c 1		
3	a 1	b 2	c 3			13	a 1	b 2	c 3		
4	a 3	b 1	c 2			14	a 1	b 2	c 3		
5	a 3	b 2	c 1			15	a 1	b 2	c 3		
6	a 2	b 3	c 1			16	a 1	b 2	c 3		
7	a 3	b 1	c 2			17	a 1	b 2	c 3		
8	a 1	b 3	c 2			18	a 1	b 2	c 3		
9	a 2	b 3	c 1			19	a 3	b 1	c 2		
10	a 2	b 3	c 1			20	a 1	b 2	c 3		

Score: 20–29

You sound like a human dynamo. You will certainly go places career-wise and your enthusiasm for your work is self-evident. If you have not yet reached the pinnacle of success, you are certainly heading in the right direction to make a take-over bid. A word of caution: you could be in danger of becoming a workaholic and a bore to others. Take things easy from time to time and you may even find your output increases.

Score: 30–45

You are fairly contented with your lot – though it would appear that with a bit more effort you could make your working day a great deal more exciting. It is unlikely that you will achieve fame and fortune in your present circumstance. Perhaps a change of location would bring back the sparkle to your eyes.

Score: 46 or over

It may be time for a change. You either need a completely different career or an entirely new approach to your current one. You must be pretty unhappy and resentful of your current working circumstances, and your attitude is no doubt reflected in the way your colleagues treat you. Why not take stock of your situation, seek career guidance and consider making a fresh start.

MALENESS, FEMALENESS AND

SOCIETY

'**W**hy must I lie beneath you? I also was made from dust, and am therefore your equal.' So protested Lilith, the wife of Adam, in ancient Hebrew scripture. If anyone imagines that feminism is new they should read the story of Joan of Arc, who was persecuted among other things for wearing men's clothes, or attend a performance of Gilbert and Sullivan's *Princess Ida*, in which the central character preaches female superiority and bans all allusions to lust and motherhood.

It is true that the debate is livelier and more insistent today than it perhaps has been at any time in the past. Women (and for that matter men) are strongly divided with respect to the proper role of women. Some think that women are naturally cut out for raising a family and providing emotional support for men. Others believe women should strive for greater respect and power in the world, compete with men in traditional male occupations, such as politics and flying aeroplanes, and that men should be persuaded to share equally in household chores and childcare.

Is it only 'butch' women who promote feminism while feminine women accept traditional sex roles? Apparently not, for research shows that femininity and feminism are almost completely independent. A person can be high on femininity and low on feminism just as easily as they can be high or low on both, allowing for all possible combinations.

A word should be said about the meaning of masculinity, versus femininity, as this concept has often been misunderstood. As used by psychologists, this quite simply refers to the average difference in personality and preferences between men and women. Using items that discriminate men and women as groups, it is possible to measure variation within each sex. There is no implication that one or the other trait is more desirable, nor any innuendo that a feminine man is necessarily gay or a masculine woman lesbian. The preference for male versus female sex partners is another separate distinction not considered here.

At first blush it might seem counter-intuitive that a woman could be both feminist and feminine. Surely, you might think, it is the tough 'macho' woman who is competitive and who strives for success within male spheres. But the fact of the matter is that men and women do differ in temperamental tendencies, in attitudes, beliefs and values. Nobody really denies the existence of these differences, *on average*; where the dispute lies between feminists and traditionalists is on the question of the origins of these differences and the extent to which political pressure should be applied to override them. Feminists think that masculinity and femininity are historical, social and political in origin, and that they can (and should) be adjusted by political measures and education (or propaganda, depending on your own position). Traditionalists believe that the differences are natural or God-given so that change is unnecessary, undesirable and probably impossible. Both sets of beliefs may be found in men as well as women, and in masculine as well as feminine people within each sex.

A case that may help to illustrate the point is that of Margaret Thatcher, who has certain masculine traits, such as dominance, determination and capacity for emotional detachment, yet would not be regarded as a feminist. In fact, many feminists were upset by her promotion of Victorian family values and what they saw as her failure to promote the cause of women. The unspoken assumption is that Lady Thatcher believes that women should get on in the world through their own individual initiative, without state support, or else they should accept the traditional wife/mother role and try to maximise its rewards. Most feminists believe that, given an unfair *status quo*, this is unreasonable and that some kind of state intervention is necessary to achieve a just society.

How do *you* stand with respect to these two important factors? Answer the following questions and find out.

I Under what circumstances would you resort to physical violence?

a To uphold your honour.
b To defend your country.
c Only to protect loved ones.

2   How do you feel about the opposite sex?

   a You prefer the company of your own sex because it is less threatening sexually.

   b You prefer the opposite sex because you feel stimulated and flirtatious.

   c You enjoy the company of men and women equally.

3   Offered a choice, which of the following lectures would interest you most?

   a Treasures of Ancient Egypt.

   b The history of European royalty.

   c The possibilities of life in outer space.

4   If reincarnation were true, how would you like to be born again?

   a A sexy and glamorous film star.

   b A talented and successful author.

   c A strong and progressive politician.

5   You are giving an interior designer a briefing. Your priority is to create a decor that is:

   a Beautiful and ornamental.

   b Elegant and uncluttered.

   c Functional and hi-tech.

6   In your opinion, do people of the opposite sex exploit each other?

   a Women are too often abused by men.

   b The wiles of women are more than a match for men.

   c Each gender makes a contribution to society.

7   Which author would you most enjoy reading?

   a Barbara Cartland.

   b Agatha Christie.

   c Ian Fleming.

8   Should a woman suppress her intelligence in order to please or impress men?

   a Yes – she has much to gain by allowing a man to feel superior.

b Occasionally – when the stakes are worthwhile, she might play his games.

c Never – fools of either sex should not be suffered gladly.

9 What type of film would you choose to see?

a A fast-moving comedy to make you ache with laughing.

b A love story which gives you a good cry.

c An anti-war movie with a powerful message to get you thinking.

10 When a heterosexual relationship is on the rocks, what is the best way to hold it together?

a Obtain professional guidance.

b Have a soul-searching session.

c For the woman to get pregnant.

11 Which science would you be most inclined to study?

a Biology.

b Physics.

c Chemistry.

12 What role do the media play to further the cause of women?

a They stimulate discussion and make women re-evaluate their roles.

b They enhance the quality of life by showing beautiful women in fantasy settings.

c None – they degrade women by treating them as sex objects.

13 What do you do when you find a huge hairy spider?

a Take fright and get someone else to dispose of it.

b Kill it – they're unpleasant creatures.

c Ignore it – spiders don't bother you.

14 The main interest a man has in a woman is her:

a Body.

b Mind.

c Soul.

15 A serious talk with a friend would be about:

a The state of the nation.

b The state of their relationship.

c The state of the test match.

16   Generally speaking, whose fault is it if a woman does not succeed in life?

   a Despite disadvantages in some spheres, a determined woman can still make it.

   b Women have only themselves to blame if they cannot make a go of life.

   c Women can never achieve their full potential while society oppresses them.

17   Which fantasy most appeals to you:

   a You make your victim submit to your will.

   b You are crowned ruler of a Pacific island.

   c You walk down the aisle of Westminster Abbey with your betrothed.

18   An employer who is faced with a man and a woman of similar qualifications should give the job to:

   a The man, who has a family to support.

   b The woman, to equalise previous injustices.

   c The person who is most likely to perform the job effectively.

19   What physical activity do you most enjoy?

   a Playing a sport such as tennis.

   b Energetic dancing.

   c Making love.

20   What do you believe is the main source of masculine and feminine behaviour?

   a Hormonal differences.

   b Social role learning.

   c A mixture of biological and social factors.

21   What do you feel when shown scenes of violence and torture at the cinema?

   a Rather nauseated.

   b A positive thrill.

   c Some ambivalence.

22   What do women get their greatest rewards from?

   a Proving that they are as good as men.

   b Raising a family.

   c Being satisfied with their own achievement.

23 There is a bad pile-up in fog on the motorway. You are most concerned about:

  a Getting out of the way to let help get through.
  b Getting a good look to see what's happened.
  c Looking the other way because blood and guts disturb you.

24 How do you think women can best overcome discrimination?

  a By organising women's groups at the workplace.
  b By proving their ability as individuals.
  c They should drop the sex war and enjoy being women.

25 If you were lending a lot of money to a person you didn't know well, how would you rely on their trustworthiness?

  a Solid collateral.
  b Reliable references.
  c Your own intuition.

26 Women envy men in particular for their:

  a Freedom.
  b Power.
  c Intellect.

27 You think comedians who make crude and near-the-knuckle jokes are:

  a The only ones worth watching.
  b Sometimes quite funny.
  c Dirty and seldom amusing.

28 What would you give a teenage girl as a stocking filler for Christmas?

  a A poster of her favourite singer.
  b A pair of lacy gloves.
  c An anti-rape whistle.

29 On a day when everything and everybody seems to be against you, the best way to cope is to:

  a Have good cry.
  b Let off steam by physical exercise.
  c Get drunk.

30 Which of these women do you most admire?

   a Margaret Thatcher.
   b Joan Collins.
   c Vanessa Redgrave.

31 What fear would be most likely to feature in your nightmares?

   a Being lost in a dark forest.
   b Losing in physical combat.
   c Being publicly disgraced.

32 Why do women have a tendency to outlive men?

   a Men are too aggressive and belligerent for the sake of their own health.
   b The lifestyle of men exposes them to more danger and stress.
   c Constitutional differences, such as rate of metabolism, make for a shorter life expectation in men.

33 You would most value a ticket to see:

   a A famous cabaret performer.
   b The Royal Ballet.
   c A world title fight.

34 What qualities should a man look for in his mate?

   a Someone who is bright and fun to be with.
   b A good sparring partner.
   c A woman who is nurturant and caring.

35 If a friend brought round his/her new puppy, you would:

   a Ignore it.
   b Cuddle and fuss over it.
   c Wonder if it's house trained.

36 What is most important for a woman to learn?

   a Cordon bleu cooking.
   b Self-defence.
   c A foreign language.

37 In an average day, what do you think about most?

   a Planning your social life.
   b Falling in love.
   c Getting ahead in your work.

38 Women have traditionally been responsible for child-rearing. Would you like:

 a A law to be passed to reverse this commitment?
 b The father to share some of this burden?
 c The natural and obvious roles to continue?

39 What kind of magazines would you browse in a waiting room?

 a Fashion/personal relationships.
 b Nature/geography.
 c Science fiction/mechanics.

40 What does women's liberation represent to you?

 a Progress at its best but ridiculous when taken to extremes.
 b A threat to men that is undermining chivalry and romance.
 c The only way for women's achievements to be recognised and appreciated.

41 If you received an invitation to a sex orgy you would respond with:

 a Great eagerness.
 b Mild amusement.
 c Total disbelief.

42 You admire a woman as a success when she is:

 a Crowned 'Miss World'.
 b Elected to political leadership.
 c Recognised as a great actress.

43 As part of a community project, your local vicar asks you to sing in the church choir. You:

 a Say you would be delighted and offer to recruit more members.
 b Say you are an atheist and can't sing.
 c Say you are busy but send a donation.

44 If a woman has young children and a career, what should she do?

 a Take the children into work with her.
 b Find a suitable 'support system' to enable her to work at least part time.
 c Give up work to devote her time to the children.

45   Visiting a glamorous major city, the first thing you do is:

  a Obtain a map and tour places of interest.
  b Head for the main shopping area.
  c Check out the night spots with a 'local'.

46   How should a woman dress?

  a To please herself.
  b To attract a man.
  c To show that she is not helpless or just a sex object.

47   Do you think it is right for children to be read stories about war?

  a Yes, we have a lot to be proud of.
  b Yes, to try and prevent future wars.
  c No, such atrocities are best forgotten.

48   How do you think a married couple should divide labour?

  a Splitting equally in all respects, both breadwinning and domestic chores.
  b Whoever is best equipped to make a career should do so, while the other provides support of whatever kind is necessary.
  c The man should go out to work while the woman looks after home and children.

49   If you were to take up painting as a hobby, what subject would you choose?

  a Scenic landscapes, such as mountains and forests.
  b Children and flower arrangements.
  c Action sports like skiing and skydiving.

50   What is your feeling about men wolf-whistling at attractive women?

  a Rather pathetic but fairly harmless.
  b It is disrespectful and insulting.
  c Any woman with a sense of humour would take it in fun and accept it as a compliment.

SCORING

	Femininity				Feminism	
	Score 0 for each	Score 1 for each	Score 2 for each		Score 2 for each	Score 1 for each	Score 0 for each
1 a	b	c		2 a	c	b
3 c	a	b		4 c	b	a
5 c	b	a		6 a	c	b
7 c	b	a		8 c	b	a
9 c	a	b		10 b	a	c
11 b	c	a		12 c	a	b
13 c	b	a		14 a	b	c
15 c	a	b		16 c	a	b
17 a	b	c		18 b	c	a
19 c	a	b		20 b	c	a
21 b	c	a		22 a	c	b
23 b	a	c		24 a	b	c
25 a	b	c		26 b	a	c
27 a	b	c		28 c	a	b
29 c	b	a		30 c	a	b
31 b	c	a		32 a	c	b
33 c	a	b		34 b	a	c
35 a	c	b		36 b	c	a
37 c	a	b		38 a	b	c
39 c	b	a		40 c	a	b
41 a	b	c		42 b	c	a
43 b	c	a		44 a	b	c
45 a	c	b		46 c	a	b
47 a	b	c		48 a	b	c
49 c	a	b		50 b	a	c
Femininity total =				Feminism total =		

Transfer your answers to the table above and then add down the columns to arrive at separate scores for femininity and feminism. Now plot these scores (which should be somewhere between 0 and 50) on the chart on page 83, showing yourself as a cross which marks your position in relation to each of the two dimensions.

Your position on this chart tells where you stand relative to the rest of the population. If your cross is right in the middle of the chart, you are average (or, if you prefer, 'normal') on both dimensions. If your cross is displaced towards the left, your personality and interests are more like those of the typical male; if you are located to the right you are more feminine. Not surprisingly, men are more likely to score as masculine and women feminine, but there is nevertheless a great deal of cross-over, and if you happen to fall on the 'wrong' side of the centreline, there is no need to worry – this does not mean that you are homosexual or mentally abnormal.

If you are towards the top of the chart, your attitudes and beliefs are in the direction of feminist, and if your cross is in the lower part of the chart, you tend more in the direction of favouring traditional sex roles. It is not for us to say which is better: the whole point is that attitudes and values vary with respect to this dimension.

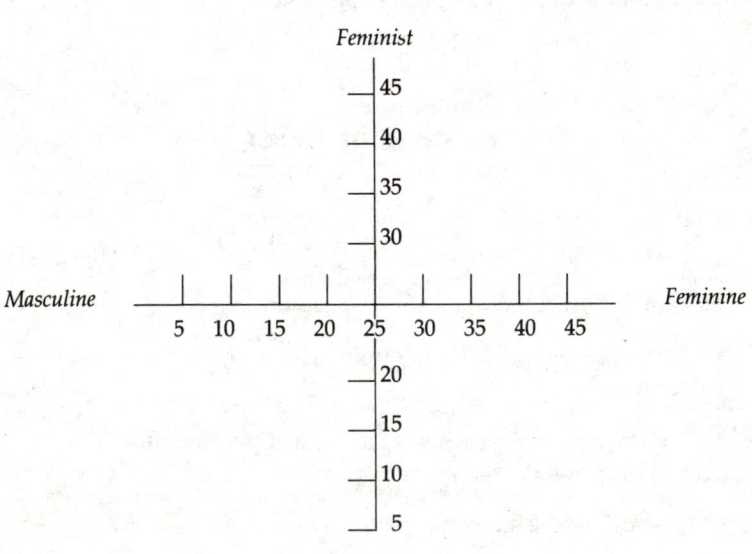

HOW IS YOUR SEX LIFE?

The question is often asked of us jokingly. Our public reply is likely to be equally flippant, yet it may start us thinking seriously about what the real answer should be. The difficulty is to know how to compare ourselves with other people, and on what yardstick to assess ourselves.

Here are five short quizzes which will help you to find out how you stand with respect to some of the factors psychologists regard as most important in sexual conduct and happiness.

I   CONFIDENCE

1   If I see someone I fancy I have no difficulty in telling them.   *True*   *False*

2   I am not ashamed to be seen in the nude.   *True*   *False*

3   Shyness often prevents me from making sexual contacts.   *True*   *False*

4   I worry a great deal whether my sexual performance will be adequate.   *True*   *False*

5   I regard myself as sexually attractive.   *True*   *False*

6   I am embarrassed to talk about sex.   *True*   *False*

7   I dress so as to disguise some part of my figure I am not happy with.   *True*   *False*

8   The size and shape of my sex organs is quite satisfactory.   *True*   *False*

9 I am anxious about my breath and body odours. *True* *False*

10 I have plenty of friends of the opposite sex. *True* *False*

Scoring

Give yourself 1 point for each 'True' answer to questions 1, 2, 5, 8 and 10, and 1 point for each 'False' answer to questions 3, 4, 6, 7 and 9.
    A total score of 4–6 is average, 0–3 is low and 7–10 is high.

2   FULFILMENT

1 Something is lacking in my love life. *True* *False*

2 My partner satisfies all my physical needs. *True* *False*

3 I can seldom relax properly during sex. *True* *False*

4 Some things I do not really enjoy I do just to please my partner. *True* *False*

5 All in all I am happy with my love life. *True* *False*

6 Love-making has become rather a boring routine. *True* *False*

7 My sexual encounters are usually intensely rewarding. *True* *False*

8 I am getting all the sex I need at the moment. *True* *False*

9 I am often left frustrated after intercourse. *True* *False*

10 I find it easy to tell my partner what I like and dislike sexually. *True* *False*

Scoring

Give yourself 1 point for each 'True' answer to questions 2, 5, 7, 8 and 10, and 1 point for each 'False' answer to questions 1, 3, 4, 6 and 9.
    A total of 4–6 is average, 0–3 is low and 7–10 is high.

3 PERMISSIVENESS

1 There is no excuse for adultery.   *True* *False*

2 Virginity is a girl's most valuable possession.   *True* *False*

3 Homosexuals should be free to live and love as they
   please.   *True* *False*

4 There is too much pornography available today.   *True* *False*

5 Teenagers should have easy access to
   contraceptives.   *True* *False*

6 Prostitution should be made legal.   *True* *False*

7 It is disturbing to see nudity on the beach.   *True* *False*

8 Masturbation is a degrading practice.   *True* *False*

9 Sex play among young children is fairly harmless.   *True* *False*

10 Mate-swapping is all right for those who enjoy it.   *True* *False*

Scoring

Give yourself 1 point for each 'True' answer to questions 3, 5, 6, 9 and
10, and 1 point for each 'False' answer to questions 1, 2, 4, 7 and 8.
   A total score of 4–6 is average, 0–3 is low and 7–10 is high.

4 LIBIDO

1 Days go by without me ever thinking about sex.   *True* *False*

2 Conditions have to be just right before I can get
   excited.   *True* *False*

3 I find myself initiating sex more than my partner.   *True* *False*

4 I am not turned on by nude pictures.   *True* *False*

5 I have a lot of exciting sexual fantasies.   *True* *False*

6 I seem to be less interested in sex than most of my
   friends. *True* *False*

7 Sex is far and away my greatest pleasure. *True* *False*

8 I get very passionate and carried away when making
   love. *True* *False*

9 I like to look at attractive people and wonder what
   they would be like as lovers. *True* *False*

10 A good book is usually more fun than sex. *True* *False*

Scoring

Give yourself 1 point for each 'True' answer to questions 3, 5, 7, 8 and
9, and 1 point for each 'False' answer to questions 1, 2, 4, 6 and 10.
   A total score of 4–6 is average, 0–3 is low, and 7–10 is high.

5 EXPLORATION

1 Orthodox sexual intercourse is quite sufficient for
   me. *True* *False*

2 It is not in my nature to remain faithful to one partner
   for life. *True* *False*

3 I sometimes play games like spanking or cross-
   dressing as a kind of foreplay. *True* *False*

4 Under no circumstances would I consider sex play
   with a member of my own sex. *True* *False*

5 Variety is the spice of love as well as life. *True* *False*

6 I could never have sex with a stranger. *True* *False*

7 The idea of oral sex is distasteful. *True* *False*

8 I might enjoy group sex if all the people were
   sufficiently appealing. *True* *False*

9 I am excited by the idea of having sex with someone
   of different race to myself. *True* *False*

10 I never make love outside of the bedroom. *True* *False*

Scoring

Give yourself 1 point for each 'True' answer to questions 2, 3, 5, 8 and 9, and 1 point for each 'False' answer to questions 1, 4, 6, 7 and 10.

A total score of 4–6 is average, 0–3 is low and 7–10 is high.

INTERPRETATION

It is not necessary to have a high *libido* in order to be satisfied in your sex life. The important thing is to find a partner who is compatible in sex drive. Much the same is true of *permissiveness*. It is an important basis on which people differ and a major potential source of conflict between a couple. Nobody can say which end of the permissive-puritan dimension is the right one, but you can be sure that you will get on better with someone who thinks like you in this respect.

Although most people regard their views as based on logic or ideals, such as religion, research shows a strong link between sex drive and permissiveness – so much so that it is difficult to measure them separately. The chances are that if you scored high on one, you will also have a high score on the other, and vice versa. People's attitudes to sex, therefore, seem to be derived in large part from their hormones rather than the rational part of their brain.

Exploration is a form of sexual behaviour which is also closely related to libido and permissiveness. People with a high sex drive like to try out different types of sexual behaviour. Since men on average have a higher sex drive than women, they also tend to be more permissive and exploratory. All your scores should, therefore, be interpreted in the light of this typical gender difference.

Confidence bears more upon happiness in sex than libido. This is a matter of social skills. It is important to take care of your personal appearance without being obsessive about it. Remember that most people are more shy than they pretend, that shyness can be very attractive when it does show, and that everyone likes compliments and feels flattered by a show of sexual interest.

Fulfilment is the direct measure of how satisfactory your sex life is. If you find yourself to be lacking in fulfilment, you may find clues as to the reason in the other scores. Perhaps you are lacking in confidence and cannot approach suitable partners or communicate with the one you love. Perhaps you and your partner differ with respect to libido, permissiveness or exploration. If you can persuade your partner to answer these questions also, you might be able to have a constructive chat about things afterwards.

14

ARE YOU SEXUALLY MATURE?

Sexual maturity is not just a matter of age. Nor is it just a matter of experience – although experience may sometimes help. Some people behave in a sensitive, sophisticated manner, displaying a sound understanding of the opposite sex and the mutual delights that may be found in love-making from the earliest days of courtship. Others blunder somewhat blindly through their sex lives, missing out on many of the more subtle yet profoundly erotic experiences and wreaking hurt, or even destruction, upon their unfortunate partners. In a sexual sense, they appear never to grow up.

Of course, the question of which modes of sexual expression are mature and which are immature is to some extent a value judgement. Some of the qualities that we associate with children – innocence, originality and a sense of fun, for example – are well worth preserving and cultivating into adulthood as far as possible. The pity is that we find youthful attributes such as these so difficult to maintain as age, care and responsibility overtake us. But other childish attributes, such as selfishness, gluttony, pride, envy, insecurity, sexual vulgarity and a lavatorial sense of humour, are better dispensed with as we grow towards adulthood. It is characteristics such as these that we call immature when they appear in older people.

The man who throws a tantrum because his wife dances closely with an attractive man at a party is equivalent to the little boy who refuses to share his toys with a visitor. The woman who judges a man by the cost of his car or the wealth of his parents is not far removed from the little girl who demands a bigger doll than her friends and accuses her father of not loving her because he cannot afford it or decides not to indulge her. It is usually easy to see these comparisons from the outside point of view – not so easy to identify childish behaviour in ourselves, especially at the time, when we are emotionally involved in it.

Is maturity versus immaturity the same thing as giving versus taking? Not exactly, though the ability and willingness to give as much as we take is an important aspect of maturity. One of the things we learn as we grow up is that there are other people in the world to be considered and that we cannot always have things entirely our own way. As we gain in maturity, we also discover progressively that the giving of pleasure to another person we love is actually one of the greatest of life's satisfactions – oddly enough, more pleasurable than the receipt of favours from others. This is because living for another person provides the long-term happiness and contentment that comes out of having a meaning in life – a purpose. And in purely utilitarian terms, the best way to persuade someone to love us deeply is to love them first; demanding greater affection and attention directly from another person is not just ineffective, it is usually counter-productive. No one finds it easy to love a selfish, demanding, attention-seeker.

When it comes to love-making, what counts most is sensitivity to the reactions of the partner – what might be called 'erotic empathy'. Some aspects of this might be developed with experience of a variety of partners, but since people are all so different in their likes and dislikes, experience with the particular partner is most important.

True sensitivity in the sexual arena means being aware of the other's mood, timing and special turn-ons – mental as well as physical. Even though we ourselves may be very aroused and ready for sex, we need to recognise that our partner may need a little bit of time to warm up. It is good policy to proceed more slowly towards intercourse than we think is really necessary for the arousal of our partner. If this amounts to a kind of teasing, all to the good, for most of our pleasures are the greater for some delay in gratification. This may even be a justification for certain practices, such as playful bondage and blindfolding, which have kinky, sadomasochistic overtones to most people but which are recognised and adopted by sexually creative people as enjoyable extensions of experience. The choice of unusual and erotic venues for sexual activity, such as forests, fields and beaches, may likewise be considered playful and romantic rather than perverted.

The use of touch should be judicious. Most people have parts of their body where they enjoy being stroked and caressed and others that are unpleasantly ticklish or irritating. The order of progression is also important; grabbing someone straight in the genitals is likely to be more of a turn-off than an erotic experience. Like tea-drinking in Japan, the slowly ordered sequence of events (ritual or ceremony) is of prime importance – consummation is just the finale.

There may be occasions when sudden, impulsive sex is appropriate, and perhaps especially exciting, but mature lovers do not use quickies as a staple diet. For an excellent overview of gourmet sexual techniques, readers could not do better than consult Dr Alex Comfort's sophisticated sex manuals, *The Joy of Sex* and *More Joy of Sex*. There are few lovers in the world who would not gain some extra degree of maturity through reading these well-deserved best-sellers.

Finally, perhaps the most important criterion of sexual maturity is recognition of the fact that one's partner is an individual person, not just an appendage, toy or piece of property. It is necessary to acknowledge that they have feelings, attitudes, and preferences that are not necessarily identical to our own or geared to our own gratification. The sexually mature person will respect their partner as well as love them.

To find out how you rate as regards sexual maturity, answer the questions below.

1   What does a sophisticated man value most in a woman?

   a A sexy figure.
   b A good homemaker.
   c Intelligence and a sense of humour.

2   What does a discriminating woman find most impressive in a man?

   a A large bank balance.
   b A fast car.
   c Good manners and consideration.

3   What is the key to having good sex?

   a Being in love.
   b A sense of humour.
   c Respect for each other.

4   What size should a man's penis be in order to satisfy a woman?

   a At least 6 inches.
   b Circumference is more important.
   c Size is totally irrelevant.

5   If a man sees an attractive woman on the other side of a crowded bar, how should he bring himself to her attention?

   a With a loud wolf whistle.
   b By positioning himself close to her and waiting for an opportunity to engage her in conversation.
   c By going up to her and introducing himself.

6 What is the biggest turn-on to an experienced lover?

a Talking dirty.
b A private strip-tease show.
c Playing sexually titillating mind games.

7 What do you do if your lover is always surrounded by admirers?

a Put the word around that they have a sexually transmitted disease.
b Make sure you are always around to show who is number one.
c Feel flattered they have chosen you from so many.

8 How often do you pay a compliment to your lover?

a Seldom – you expect them to shower you with compliments.
b When they are looking fantastic.
c When they have achieved something worthwhile.

9 How do you tell when a person is sexually mature?

a They have reached puberty.
b When they lose their virginity.
c They have learned to regard sex as a pleasure, not a threat.

10 Your partner enjoys deep, French kissing but you find it distasteful. You:

a Bite their tongue and pretend it was an accident.
b Say you are not fond of kissing that way.
c Make love-making so exciting in other ways, they won't even miss it.

11 The only satisfactory way to finish sex is for:

a The man to have an orgasm.
b Both to achieve an orgasm.
c Both to feel totally relaxed and in harmony – whether an orgasm has been achieved or not.

12 Who is responsible for contraception?

a You both trust to fate.
b It is up to the woman to ensure she does not get pregnant.
c Both partners should take a conscious decision about whether to have children.

13 When you have been with your partner for some time and the edge seems to be wearing off your sex life, do you?

- **a** Panic, in case they go off with someone else.
- **b** Go out and buy some equipment from a sex shop.
- **c** Choose an erotic movie to watch together.

14 If the man loses his erection due to drinking or over-excitement, what should the woman do?

- **a** Get angry and call him useless.
- **b** Try not to show her disappointment.
- **c** Cuddle up to him, waiting a while before working on him.

15 Are men and women the same when it comes to fears of sexual performance?

- **a** Women don't enjoy sex as much as men, so they are naturally not so good at it.
- **b** A woman can always fake it – it's the man who can be ridiculed.
- **c** Both care as much as the other about not disappointing their lover.

16 Does the number of positions you can make love in determine great sex?

- **a** Only good athletes make great lovers.
- **b** Not necessarily but new positions should always be tried.
- **c** Providing you are both very sensual, the missionary position can be all you need.

17 A person has reached the height of sexual accomplishment when they:

- **a** Have had more than a hundred lovers.
- **b** Are steeped in erotic culture and have studied all the love manuals.
- **c** Have learned how to satisfy one lover completely.

18 Under what circumstances might you cheat on your lover?

- **a** If they were unfaithful to you.
- **b** If they would never discover your indiscretion.
- **c** If you met someone you were wildly attracted to.

19 With a new lover, the cool way to hold their interest would be:

   a To get in touch with their last lover to discover their habits and preferences.

   b To contact them after a suitable interval – say 10 days.

   c To phone them as soon as you feel the need to keep the passion burning.

20 You are sexually propositioned by a very attractive underage person. You:

   a Jump at the chance and hope you won't be discovered.

   b Tell their parents and suggest they punish them so it won't happen again.

   c Reassure them of their attractiveness but point out your responsibility to forego the pleasure.

21 How do you behave when you are feeling sexy and your partner is not in the mood?

   a Accuse them of being inadequate or unfaithful.

   b Go to sleep and hope things will improve in the morning.

   c Seduce them artfully.

22 Would you contemplate a long-term relationship with a person much older than yourself?

   a No way – you don't fancy pushing someone around in a wheelchair when you are still young.

   b It's only acceptable if the man is older – women 'go off' faster.

   c You would appreciate the experience they could bring to the relationship.

23 Do you think sex is directly linked with romance?

   a You'd rather have pure romance any day.

   b Good sex only follows a romantic interlude.

   c The two are indistinguishable if you love the person you have sex with.

24 After making love you usually:

   a Fall asleep immediately.

   b Go to the bathroom and wash.

   c Continue to caress your partner lovingly.

25   Your lover suggests you play a bondage game. You:

   a Refuse outright and tell them they are sick.
   b Agree to play and then tell all their friends about it in the pub.
   c Enter into the spirit, making sure it is only in fun and does not get out of hand.

26   Booking into a hotel for a weekend with his lover, a man should:

   a Make a scene if there are only twin-bedded rooms.
   b Sign in as Mr and Mrs Smith and wink broadly at the receptionist.
   c Make his lover feel comfortable with the situation and excitingly special.

27   At the office party you have a bit too much to drink and end up having sex with a married colleague. The next day at work you:

   a Can't remember anything because you were too drunk.
   b Feel ashamed and embarrassed and avoid seeing your colleague.
   c Greet your colleague in a friendly, businesslike way and in a moment alone say what a fun evening you had but you have no wish to make a habit of it.

28   What would be a good meal to have before love-making?

   a A banquet with all the trimmings to make you soporific.
   b A hot curry to get the fires burning.
   c Succulent tropical fruits and tit-bits consumed while languishing in bed.

29   Is there a universal erogenous zone for all men and women?

   a Most people like kissing best.
   b Yes, breasts in women and genitals in men.
   c Every individual is different in having special areas of their body which give them intense pleasure.

30   What is the most erotic way to make love?

   a To get turned on quickly so you can get it over with and do more important things.
   b To lie in each other's arms and talk of love.
   c To spend hours working on your partner as a preamble with massage oils, sensual music and candlelight.

31 What gives some men a special quality that makes them more attractive to women than other men are?

   a Expensive clothes and cologne.
   b Their eyes and the way they move.
   c Their ability to make women feel at ease and fascinating.

32 Apart from obvious physical attributes, why does one particular woman get more male attention than others?

   a Because she is cheap and easy to get into bed.
   b Because she dresses provocatively.
   c Because she knows how to relax around men and oozes confidence and charm.

33 In which of the following venues would you most enjoy seducing your lover?

   a At home, in bed.
   b On holiday, in a luxury hotel.
   c In an unusual and exotic setting – such as a deserted cove on the beach.

34 How can you tell if a person really loves you?

   a By asking them several times a day.
   b By the things they do for you.
   c By the way your bodies fuse in unison when you make love.

35 What is the best way to keep passion alive in a long-term relationship?

   a Spending money on sexy underwear.
   b Always being available when your lover wants sex.
   c By being sexually imaginative and making your lover feel loved and desired.

36 When you and your lover have a row, it is generally:

   a A time for bitter recriminations.
   b Held over for hours, sometimes days.
   c A flash of temper, made up in bed.

37 If you were asked to nominate your best friend who would it be?

   a Your mother.
   b A same sex childhood playmate.
   c Your lover.

38 Your partner confesses that they have had sex with someone else but reassures you that it did not mean anything to them and certainly does not affect your relationship. You:

   a Walk out on them.
   b Say you forgive them but constantly refer back to the incident bitterly.
   c Thank them for trusting you with the confidence, even if it gives you no particular thrill.

39 You are witness to a group of young men sexually annoying a pretty young woman. You:

   a Say, 'boys will be boys' and leave them to it.
   b Make an issue of it offering violence.
   c Suggest to the boys that they might be a lot more successful with girls if they did not gang up and harass them.

40 What advice would you give to a young girl, reaching the age of consent?

   a Make sure she has a ring on her finger before she gives away her virginity.
   b Wait for Mr Right to come along.
   c Always be prepared to give to your partner and don't expect something in return.

SCORING

Add up the number of 'a', 'b' and 'c' answers that you gave and award yourself 1 point for each 'a', 2 for each 'b' and 3 for each 'c'. This will give you a score of somewhere in the range of 40–120. These scores may be interpreted as follows:

Score: 100—120

You appear to be a very mature and sophisticated lover, with a full appreciation of erotic nuance and the needs of your partner. There is little that anyone can teach you about sexual manners, and you should have little difficulty in initiating and maintaining satisfying relationships with members of the opposite sex.

Score: 80—99

You are reasonably competent and adult in the conduct of your love life and your behaviour towards people of the opposite sex. However, you might improve slightly upon your sensitivity and manners and a look back over the answers that you have given to the quiz might be of assistance in this respect.

Score: 60—77

There are definite signs of immaturity in your attitudes and behaviour in the area of love and sex. Even though you might disagree with some of the values inherent in the scoring criteria, this quiz will hopefully set you thinking and perhaps help you to reconstruct your love-life positively and modify your dealings with the opposite sex to the benefit of all concerned.

Score: 40—59

You are either very young or very naïve where partnerships and the opposite sex are concerned. A few people might initially be attracted by your childish, egocentric approach, but the majority of partners would soon identify you as a boorish individual and an unsatisfactory lover. Perhaps you were just playing around with the quiz; if not, you should step back and take a long, hard look at yourself. If that does not point the way to improvement, you would be well advised to seek the services of a professional counsellor.

ARE MEN LESS MATURE THAN WOMEN?

It is often said that girls mature faster than boys. This is true in the physical sense, in that girls reach puberty a year or so earlier than boys. In the mental or emotional sense it also appears true that girls develop responsible, considerate attitudes towards sexual relationships earlier and more readily than boys.

Perhaps this arises out of necessity – after all, sex can be treated as a game or sport by men for the whole of their lives, being kept separate from work and even family to some extent. This is not so easy for women who are bound to bear the brunt (as well as the babies) in matters of reproduction and family and are, therefore, inclined to take the whole matter of sexual relationships more seriously.

Very generally speaking, women tend to put a higher premium on stable, loving relationships, while men are more inclined towards uncommitted, lustful, sex for the sake of sex with a variety of partners. The female pattern, because it is further removed from the selfish hedonism of the child, may quite reasonably be described as more mature.

Since long-term devotion, consideration for the partner, and probably altruism in general, are more in the nature of women than men, it will be no surprise to discover that, on average, women gain higher scores on this quiz than men. Although an attempt was made to construct this quiz on a unisex basis, it was not possible to override this difference between men and women entirely. On the one hand, this may be taken as proof of the feminist assertion that men are chauvinistic; on the other hand, it may persuade the woman whose partner comes out as much less mature than herself to view him in a more charitable light – after all, he is probably fairly typical of his gender.

15

TEST YOUR SEXUAL IQ

How much do you know about sex? Enough to have two or three children, you might say; or as much as the next person. If so, then it is not necessarily anything to be proud of, for despite all the publicity given to sex education in schools, most people remain remarkably ignorant as regards the facts about sex. This is especially true of Britain: surveys have shown that British schoolchildren know less about sex than almost any other European country except Ireland. The Scandinavian and other north European nations seem better at educating their children on sexual matters.

Since Victorian times, medical scientists have learned a great deal about sex. Famous landmarks have been the seven-volume *Studies in the Pyschology of Sex* by Havelock Ellis, written about the turn of the century, and the monumental surveys of the typical sexual behaviour of American men and women by Alfred Kinsey and his colleagues in the 1940s and 1950s. More recently, there are the noteworthy studies by William Masters and Virginia Johnson on the physiology of sexual arousal and orgasm, and the sex therapy programmes that have been derived from information provided by these researchers.

But although scientists have learned much about sexual behaviour, not too much of this has filtered down to politicians and legislators, let alone the person in the street. Masturbation has ceased to be regarded as a horribly deviant, pathological act and the cause of most physical and mental illnesses, partly in recognition of its near universal occurrence. But oral sex, which surveys show is also enjoyed by the vast majority of the population, is still illegal and subject to severe penalties in many parts of the world, including certain areas of the USA. Before Pierre Trudeau became Prime Minister of Canada, men in that country were given life imprisonment for having anal intercourse with their wives, usually on the basis of her testimony following a marital dispute. Oddly, anal sex is still illegal in Britain despite its legalisation for consenting adult men. Laws like these seem hopelessly out of touch with what actually happens in the bedrooms of Anglo-American couples, with the result that the majority of the population are technically deemed to be criminals on the basis of their sexual behaviour.

If legislators seem ignorant as regards sex, the average man or woman in the street is often equally so. Any doctor can relate stories of patients whose fertility problems or unwanted pregnancies could be traced to profound ignorance of the rudiments of sex. There are couples who think that twice a year is a high frequency of intercourse, or who think that semen has to be deposited in the navel for pregnancy to occur. There are women who put their oral contraceptives in their vagina and others who swallow their spermicidal pessaries. There are men who prick the end of their condom with a pin to let the air bubble out, or who push it inside their female partner believing it to be a diaphragm. A surprising number of people believe that normal intercourse and/or childbirth is anal rather than vaginal.

Scientists who try to collect information about sexual practices by surveys have to take account of the fact that many people do not understand the questions properly. In a recent survey done in the USA to find out if women married to uncircumcised men were more prone to cancer of the womb, a large sample of women was interviewed, and asked, among other things, whether their husbands were circumcised. A meeting was then held to discuss how the results should be analysed and one of the psychologists raised the question, 'But did these women *know* whether their husband was circumcised or not?' Loud laughter ensued from other members of the committee, who could not conceive that the word 'circumcision' would be misunderstood by anyone in this age of enlightenment. However, the psychologist finally persuaded his colleagues to do a follow-up survey to determine what the wives thought circumcision meant. This turned out to be an eye opener: many women had no idea what the word meant, and quite a few thought it had something to do with castration. Others knew what it meant but had never seen their husbands in the nude and, therefore, were not in a position to report on whether or not they were circumcised. As a result, the whole study had to be repeated with interviewees being given more explicit guidance as to what circumcision meant.

Although today there are many books about sex, ranging from scientific reports to how-to-do-it manuals, it is not clear that these are widely read or remembered. At a recent divorce hearing in Wales, the judge summed up a long and distressing hearing with the opinion that 'if only the wife in this case had bothered to read the sex manuals available to her, and if the husband had been more patient and understanding, this case would never have reached the court'.

Similarly, in a lecture to the Law Society by a distinguished barrister, it was argued that serious works on sex, such as Kinsey and Masters and Johnson, should be compulsory reading for all magistrates. Indeed, magistrates and judges often seem out of touch with the sexual experience of normal people, as when a rape victim is deemed promiscuous because she has had three or four male lovers in the course of her life, or when a man is described as perverted because several *Penthouse* magazines were found at his house.

Despite all the evidence of sexual ignorance within the population and the problems that may stem from it, there is still heated debate in society as to whether or not sex education should be permitted in schools. Opponents of sex education claim that it is best left to the parents to do in the home. Yet it has become progressively clear that parents are generally unable or unwilling to provide adequate sex education for their children – the embarrassment factor is too great, and they often have insufficient knowledge to impart.

Then there is the argument as to what kind of sex education should be given. Should it concentrate on the facts of reproduction, sexual 'plumbing', and practical considerations, such as contraception and sexually transmitted diseases, or should it be focused on emotional factors, relationships, marriage, family and divorce? Others would want sex education to emphasise moral and ethical considerations, or they would prefer it to be propaganda directed against promiscuity, illegitimate pregnancy and the spread of venereal disease. Whatever formal sex education is given, it has to compete against the very powerful forces of peer group or street learning – what some would call 'gutter education'. These uncensored, uninhibited sources of information will always remain potent influences (perhaps second in importance only to personal experience). Fortunately, there are signs that they are becoming a little more accurate within the relatively permissive climate of today.

Here is an opportunity for you to assess your own knowledge of sex. Select one answer for each of the questions that follow, and check your score against the key at the end.

1 What position for intercourse is most common in tribal societies?

   a Rear entry ('doggy style').

   b Face-to-face, male above ('missionary').

   c Face-to-face, female above ('Roman ride').

2 What is the main cause of orgasm difficulty in women?

   a Anxiety.
   b Religious guilt.
   c Insufficient arousal.

3 The equivalent, in a woman, of a man's penis is:

   a The vagina.
   b The vulva.
   c The clitoris.

4 A man's vasectomy prevents his:

   a Ejaculation.
   b Fertility.
   c Potency.

5 Which gender has the highest proportion of committed homosexuals?

   a Men.
   b Women.
   c About the same.

6 Which hormone is most important in determining a woman's sex drive?

   a Oestrogen.
   b Progesterone.
   c Testosterone.

7 AIDS is most likely to be caught by:

   a Performing anal sex on a man (homosexual insertion).
   b Having anal sex performed on oneself, whether male or female ('passive' anal intercourse).
   c Vaginal intercourse.

8 People who have lots of sexual fantasies are usually:

   a Perverted.
   b Creative.
   c Frustrated.

9 A child's sex is determined by:

   a The mother.
   b The father.
   c The two parents equally.

10 The average length of a man's penis, when fully erect, is:

   a 6 inches.
   b 8 inches.
   c 10 inches.

11 Kegel exercises are intended to:

   a Increase the length of a man's penis.
   b Increase the muscle control of a woman's vagina.
   c Strengthen the buttocks to improve thrust.

12 Which of these sexually transmitted diseases is most difficult to cure:

   a Syphilis.
   b Genital herpes.
   c Gonorrhea.

13 About how many sperm does a healthy man produce in a day?

   a Seventy.
   b Seventy thousand.
   c Seventy million.

14 The test-tube baby procedure is applicable when:

   a The husband's sperm count is too low.
   b The wife's fallopian tubes are blocked.
   c The wife has had a hysterectomy.

15 Which sexual variation is most common in males?

   a Sadomasochism.
   b Necrophilia.
   c Urolagnia.

16 The majority of prostitutes are:

   a Forced by poverty.
   b Lesbians.
   c Neither of the above.

17 As a woman approaches orgasm her clitoris:

   a Retracts under its hood.
   b Sticks out prominently.
   c Produces a fluid emission.

18   What are the dangers of intercourse during a woman's period?

  a Infection.
  b 'Knotting' of the penis.
  c None especially.

19   By what method is it easiest for most women to have orgasm?

  a Intercourse.
  b Masturbation.
  c Horse-riding.

20   Where is the Grafenberg spot?

  a At the back of the neck.
  b Inside the vagina (upper side).
  c Between the anus and the vagina.

21   The practice in some societies for the father to experience sympathetic labour pains is called:

  a Frottage.
  b Flanquette.
  c Couvade.

22   What is the approximate failure rate of the IUD (coil)?

  a Zero – it's perfectly safe.
  b 2% of women get pregnant per year.
  c 10% get pregnant per year.

23   Where do most child-molestations take place?

  a Out of doors.
  b In cars.
  c In the child's home.

24   What proportion of women develop a 'sex flush' (reddening of the body front) during sexual intercourse:

  a 25%.
  b 50%.
  c 75%.

25   At what age is it possible for a boy to have an erection?

  a Before birth.
  b From birth.
  c From puberty.

26 The most common theme in the sex fantasies of men is:

 a Rape.
 b Group sex.
 c Homosexuality.

27 Mate-swapping ('swinging') tends to occur in couples who are:

 a Generally irresponsible as citizens and parents.
 b Dissatisfied with each other and about to get divorced.
 c Stable, happy and otherwise well-balanced.

28 About what proportion of women report multiple orgasm as a regular occurrence?

 a 15%.
 b 35%.
 c 55%.

29 Which practice in the mother is most dangerous to an unborn child?

 a Exercise.
 b Sexual intercourse.
 c Smoking.

30 About what proportion of young couples use oral sex in their foreplay (at least in Anglo-American countries today)?

 a 20%.
 b 50%.
 c 80%.

31 What is the most prevalent type of incest?

 a Brother/sister.
 b Mother/son.
 c Father/daughter.

32 What position of intercourse is most likely to result in pregnancy?

 a Missionary.
 b 'Doggy'.
 c Female superior.

33 During orgasm the heart rate is likely to go as high as:

 a 140 beats per minute.

b 160 beats per minute.
c 180 beats per minute.

34   What is the most popular practice between lesbian women?

a Using a dildo.
b Cunnilingus.
c Anal stimulation.

35   Female orgasm during intercourse occurs most reliably in:

a Apes in the wild.
b Primitive African tribes.
c Industralised human society.

36   The majority of human societies are:

a Monogamous (one man, one wife).
b Polygynous (one man, several wives).
c Polyandrous (one woman, several husbands).

37   Roughly how many different partners does the average British man have in his lifetime?

a 2.
b 7.
c 45.

38   At what age does the typical British girl first have intercourse?

a 16.
b 18.
c 20.

39   Premenstrual tension is due to:

a Excessive psychological worries.
b Hormonal factors.
c Nothing – it's just a myth.

40   The average frequency of intercourse in young married couples (according to American surveys) is:

a Once a week.
b Three times a week.
c Six times a week.

SCORING

Correct answers are as follows:

1   b It is a myth that so-called primitive peoples favour the 'animal' rear entry position for intercourse. As with Europeans, a variety of positions are used, but the face-to-face (male on top) position is most common. This became known as 'missionary' position because Victorian missionaries used to try to persuade the natives to abandon all others in favour of it.

2   c Most orgasm difficulty in women seems to result from the fact that the average female arousal pattern is slower than that of males. Evidence implicating anxiety and guilt is slight.

3   c The clitoris is a penis equivalent in embryological terms. The penis develops out of tissue that would become a clitoris in the absence of male hormones, and male hormones given to women cause enlargement of the clitoris. Like the penis, the clitoris is the main origin of the neurological wiring for orgasm.

4   b Vasectomy just eliminates sperm from the ejaculate – the carrier bulk remains, as does sex drive and the full functioning of intercourse.

5   a About 4 or 5% of men are exclusively attracted to their own sex throughout life in any time and culture, compared with only about 1–2% of women who are exclusively lesbian. However, it is likely that a higher proportion of women have some bisexual capacity.

6   c 'Male' hormones, produced in small quantities by the adrenal glands in women, appear to be responsible for most of the sex drive.

7   b Recipient anal intercourse is the most dangerous activity as regards the risk of HIV transmission. Apparently, the virus may be carried in the semen. It is also possible that the intrusion of foreign organic matter is a direct shock to the immune system, increasing the chances of AIDS. The use of condoms is therefore recommended, especially in anal intercourse.

8 b Amount of fantasy is a good measure of libido, and this in turn is known to relate to creative energy in general.

9 b The sex of a baby is decided by the chromosome in the father's sperm – either X (female) or Y (male).

10 a Any other impression is probably a result of boasting.

11 b Devised by the physician Arnold Kegel in 1952, originally for the treatment of incontinence, these exercises are designed to increase awareness and control of the pubococcygous (PC) muscle that runs alongside the vaginal opening. These exercises are most useful if the woman's PC muscle has poor tone or has been stretched in childbirth.

12 b Genital herpes is caused by a virus and therefore cannot be treated with antibiotics. Treatments for its containment, which shorten the duration of attack and reduce the frequency of recurrence, are becoming available however.

13 c Sociobiologists regard this as prototypic of male dominance struggles. Seventy million sperm compete for just one egg.

14 b The technical term is 'ovum transplantation'. The mother's egg is removed from her ovary, fertilised in a dish by sperm from the father, and then implanted in the uterus (thus by-passing the blocked fallopian tube).

15 a Various sadomasochistic practices are quite common as a male variation. In fact, role-playing games that focus on dominance and submission are very common in the normal population of both men and women. Necrophilia (sexual interest in corpses) and urolagnia ('water sports') are much less common.

16 c Prostitutes are more often motivated by wealth or glamour than by fear of starvation, and few are lesbian in orientation. Some even enjoy sex with their clients, though they are usually only orgasmic with their own partners.

17 a Tumescence (swelling) of the clitoris occurs during the excitement phase; just prior to orgasm, the clitoris turns under 180° and retracts into its hood so that it can no longer be seen. Fluid emission sometimes occurs, but the clitoris is not involved.

18 c There are no real medical objections to having sex during menstruation.

19 b Many women who have difficulty having orgasm during intercourse are able to achieve satisfaction by masturbation, either manually or with the aid of a vibrator. Horse-riding may produce sexual excitement but it is seldom the preferred way of obtaining orgasm.

20 b Some women are particularly excited by stimulation of a small zone on the roof of the vagina about halfway between the pubic bone and the cervix. This may produce orgasm accompanied by an emission of fluid resembling prostate secretions from the urethra.

21 c In some Basque and South American societies, the father goes through a ritual sympathetic labour that is supposed magically to prevent delivery complications for the mother.

22 b Abstinence is the only foolproof technique of contraception.

23 c In more than half of all cases of child molestation, the man is known to the child as a friend, relative or acquaintance and little or no force is involved. About half of the contacts occur in the home of the adult or the child, a quarter out of doors, and the rest mostly in cars, theatres or schools.

24 a Masters and Johnson found a mottling of the skin during the excitement phase of intercourse in about a quarter of both their male and female subjects.

25 a Erections have been observed when a male child is still in the womb.

26 b Group sex appears as the central theme in about a third of the fantasies of men; rape and homosexuality each occur in less than 10% of fantasies.

27 c Mate-swappers usually have stable relationships and show little evidence of psychopathology or deviancy in other areas of life.

28   a Multiple orgasm remains only as a potential for the majority of women.

29   c The dangers of excessive exercise and sexual activity during pregnancy are small compared with the damage that smoking does to the developing fetus.

30   c Oral sex is so common that it should be regarded as a normal part of love-making, despite its illegality in many countries.

31   a Brother/sister sexual experimentation is so common that experts are divided as to how seriously to regard it.

32   a When the man is on top the semen is less likely to run out again before fertilisation has occurred. However, pregnancy often occurs with the other positions also; the differences are not great.

33   c This rate is quite often reached in both men and women and being aware of the other's racing heart may be the easiest way for a person to know if their partner has reached orgasm.

34   b Oral and manual stimulation are favoured by lesbians. Less than 20% of lesbians use dildos; in fact, some disapprove because of their male connotation.

35   c Contrary to myth, modern Western women have more orgasms than females in groups that are thought of as closer to nature.

36   b The majority of human societies permit men to have more than one wife at a time. Only about 15% insist on monogamy, and polyandry is extremely rare.

37   b This average conceals a great deal of variation. Homosexual men usually have a higher partner turnover (at least they did so before the advent of AIDS).

38   a Roughly 50% of girls have had intercourse by the age of 16, according to modern Anglo–American surveys.

39   b Although the amount of distress varies from one woman to another, phases of irritability, depression, anxiety, hostility and accident proneness are much more common about three or four days before the onset of menstruation and they are undoubtedly related to hormone cycles.

40 **b** British figures are much the same. But again there is such enormous variation from one couple to another that averages are virtually meaningless.

Now add up the total number of questions that you answered correctly to arrive at a sexual IQ score of between 0 and 40.

Score: 30–40

A very impressive performance. If you are as warm and considerate as a lover as you are sophisticated and knowledgable about sex your partner should be a very happy person.

Score: 20–29

This is a fair score but you might like to learn more. Reading this quiz and studying the correct answers is not a bad start.

Score: 10–19

Your knowledge of sex is short of satisfactory. You have a responsibility to yourself and your partner to gen up a bit on the facts of life before serious mistakes are made.

Score: 0–9

If this is your real score and not your idea of a joke, then you must have led an extremely sheltered life. Even if you are committed to a life of chastity, you have a responsibility to know more about the world than this.

16

WHAT KIND OF LOVER ARE YOU?

I t is easier to say 'I love you' than to know precisely what we mean by it, and even more difficult to know what our partner means when he or she replies, 'I love you too'. For the truth is, there are many different types of love and it is hard to know whether our own experience of it corresponds with that of anyone else.

Several systems for classifying love have been proposed, but the best-researched one is that of Canadian sociologist John Lee, described in his book *The Colors of Love* (1975). His analysis was based on people's answers to a lengthy questionnaire covering all aspects of their relationships – how they began, how soon they had sex, whether jealousy was strongly felt, the nature and frequency of arguments, break-ups and reunions, and so on. His major finding was that love could be separated into three 'primaries' which appear in various mixtures (hence the analogy with colour). Lee's work is highly technical and couched in Graeco-Latin terminology, but little is lost by describing the three major types of love as follows:

- *Passionate:* love that is romantic, obsessional, strongly emotional, and characterised by immediate physical attraction, and a need for close contact and intimacy. It is compulsive, elusive and transient, involving trauma, turmoil and tears.

- *Playful:* love that is free of commitment, fun-based and hedonistic. This may be pleasurable and exciting and is less associated with negative emotions, such as jealousy and despair. It is likely to be casual and temporary, but is relinquished without regret.

- *Practical:* love that is realistic, companionate and concerned with contractual responsibilities and role-sharing. It is long term and devoid of passion, though warm affection, understanding and loyalty may well be present.

Of course, we may experience all three of these with different people at different times of our life, and a relationship with a particular person may change from one category to another, for example, beginning on a playful basis, then becoming passionate and perhaps eventually practical (especially after marriage). But there are also individual differences as regards preferences and the frequency with which these types of love will occur to us. Men more often seek playful relationships while women tend to be more practical, but passionate love strikes men and women about equally and is often seen by the lovers themselves as a bolt from the blue that is beyond rational control.

Generally speaking, we are happier with a partner who construes the relationship in similar terms to ourselves. If the two partners have widely disparate approaches to love, misunderstandings are inevitable. For example, a playful lover may resent a practical lover for trying to trap him/her into a relationship while the latter accuses the former of being lustful, irresponsible and lacking in respect. The passionate lover demands immediate intimacy, while the practical lover maintains that love is more firmly founded if sex is postponed. Two practical lovers probably have the best chance of a permanent relationship, while two playful lovers will often split after a brief encounter. It is therefore of interest to identify your own characteristic love style.

These questions are designed to reveal what kind of lover you are. Choose one answer only to each question, the one that best applies to you. There are no right or wrong answers; it is just a matter of preference.

1 Which do you rate as most important?

    a Love.
    b Sex.
    c Marriage.

2 What sort of party most appeals to you?

    a One with lots of influential guests.
    b Soft lighting, music and gardens to roam in.
    c A crazy group where anything goes.

3 How many sex partners do you have?

    a One at a time.
    b Two or more at once.
    c Sometimes none, when there is no one special.

4 Where would you seek to find a new partner?

    a A computer date or marriage bureau.
    b An overseas holiday.
    c Parties and discos.

5   Whose opinion counts for the most with respect to your relationship?

   a Your relatives and neighbours.
   b Your friends and workmates.
   c Your own and your partner's.

6   Which birthday present would you most appreciate?

   a Perfume or cologne.
   b An erotic video.
   c An attractive table-lamp.

7   How long would you expect your love to last?

   a As long as you ignite a spark in each other.
   b As long as you can bear each other.
   c Forever.

8   Which quality do you find most appealing in the opposite sex?

   a Considerate and reliable.
   b Good-looking and charismatic.
   c Sexy and humorous.

9   How would you address your lover?

   a By his/her first name.
   b By a pet name.
   c A standard term of endearment, such as 'darling' or 'dearest'.

10   Where would you prefer to make love?

   a In front of a mirror.
   b In bed at night.
   c In a secluded forest.

11   If you saw your lover embracing someone passionately, how would you feel?

   a Jealous and angry.
   b Intrigued and slightly titillated.
   c Concerned for your future.

12   How do you deal with disagreements?

   a Discuss the matter sensibly and arrive at a compromise.

b Lie low for a few days until the argument blows over.

c Have a flaming row and make up in bed.

13 What would you do if your partner had to go abroad for a month without you?

a Pine by the telephone.

b Redecorate your home.

c Contact old flames to find some action.

14 How do you view sexual intercourse?

a Exciting and pleasurable.

b The ultimate expression of love.

c A means of procreation.

15 If you won a great deal of money in a lottery, how would you spend it?

a Take your lover to a paradise island.

b Buy a penthouse flat with sauna, Jacuzzi and pool.

c Celebrate with the family and invest the rest.

16 Meeting someone to whom you are magnetically attracted, you:

a Have a brief, sensational affair.

b Dream about them every waking hour.

c Vow to forget them so you don't jeopardise your current relationship.

17 If you were to prepare a special at-home supper for your lover, what would it be?

a A healthy well-balanced meal.

b Camembert, grapes and red wine.

c Coq au vin by candlelight.

18 Where would you shop for underwear for yourself or your partner?

a Mail order through a sexy magazine.

b A good-value department store.

c A designer boutique.

19 What is the ideal bed for yourself and your lover?

a Twin beds with firm mattresses.

b A four-poster bed with a lace canopy.

c A water-bed and a music system with stereo controls.

20   Ideally, how often would you like to see your partner?

    a Every available moment.
    b Evenings and weekends.
    c Holidays and social functions.

21   Where would you like to be married?

    a In a remote, ancient, village chapel.
    b On a yacht in the Mediterranean.
    c In the church you always attend.

22   Your partner reveals a penchant for a slightly unorthodox sexual practice. You:

    a Are delighted to experiment.
    b Make him/her promise not to hurt you.
    c Tell him/her to seek professional help.

23   You are feeling unwell and your partner wants to make love. You:

    a Go to bed before they do and feign sleep.
    b Go through with making love and feel better for doing it.
    c Give them a cuddle and ask them to wait till morning.

24   What would you do if your partner had an alcohol or drug problem?

    a Be sympathetic and try to support them personally.
    b Put them in touch with a helpline and leave home.
    c See your doctor for advice about the best professional help.

25   Which of the following do you think is the best way to keep a relationship from falling apart?

    a Buying expensive presents.
    b Having children.
    c Showing consideration.

26   What is the most important day of the year for you to be with your partner?

    a Your birthday.
    b New Year's eve.
    c Christmas day.

27   Your idea of a good lover is someone who:

    a Can be relied upon as a friend.

b Is deeply in love with you.

c Knows every sexual position.

28 If your lover confessed to having had a homosexual relationship before you met, how would you feel?

a Fascinated.

b Betrayed.

c Disgusted.

29 If you have been dating your partner for over two years do you:

a Feel it's time for a change.

b Hope it will last.

c Suggest that marriage is the obvious next step.

30 On discovering your partner is having an affair, you:

a Turn a blind eye and hope that it will be a passing fancy.

b Invite them both to dinner for a civilised evening.

c Stage a dramatic 'showdown'.

31 If your partner found you too demanding sexually you would:

a Coax them on to greater things.

b Take on another lover.

c Sublimate your desires.

32 Suppose you enjoy making love with your partner but are seldom completely satisfied. What would you do?

a Teach them precisely what gives you pleasure.

b Leave relevant literature lying around the house.

c See a marriage guidance counsellor together.

33 How often would you offer to massage your partner?

a On holidays when you are both relaxed.

b When you want to turn them on.

c Only if they needed massage therapeutically.

34 When do you laugh together?

a When there is a good comedian on TV.

b When having a few drinks with friends.

c At unexpected moments, out of sheer delight.

35 How do you think you would cope if your partner died suddenly? You would:

    a Fall into deep despair, remembering all you had done together.

    b Force yourself to form a new relationship quickly.

    c Immerse yourself in funeral arrangements and check your financial security.

36 What aspect of your relationship do you value most?

    a Good times and sexual frolics.

    b Companionship and shared responsibility.

    c The fusion of body and soul.

37 What are the main reasons you quarrel?

    a Money and the number of outings you go on together.

    b Your partner does not pay you sufficient attention.

    c Your partner hems you in and encroaches on personal freedom.

38 How do you regard sex with your partner?

    a Joyful.

    b Orgiastic.

    c A duty.

39 As you spend more time together, you regard your partner with an increasing amount of:

    a Understanding and tolerance.

    b Intimacy and involvement.

    c Boredom and restlessness.

40 If an important-looking letter arrived for your lover while they were out, you would:

    a Try to contact them.

    b Open it and read the contents.

    c Place it in a prominent position where he/she would find it.

41 When you go out to a restaurant alone with your partner, what do you talk about?

    a Your plans to go places with them.

    b Domestic problems that require attention.

    c Any topic that is scintillating.

42 Who is the most influential figure in your partner's life?

   a You.

   b His/her boss.

   c His/her mother.

43 If your lover continuously broke promises and let you down, you would:

   a Teach him/her a lesson he/she would not forget.

   b Get fed up and issue him/her with an ultimatum.

   c Always forgive him/her when you see him/her smile.

44 Which of these traits would you find most unacceptable in your partner?

   a Bad manners.

   b Lack of honesty.

   c Reckless behaviour.

45 An old flame rings you from out of the blue while your partner is in the room. You:

   a Tell the old flame you are spoken for now and don't wish to make your lover jealous.

   b Ask your partner to excuse you and take the phone next door so you can flirt.

   c Invite him/her to visit you one afternoon with his/her new partner.

46 Prolonged foreplay prior to love-making is:

   a An unnecessary delay.

   b An unusual occurrence.

   c An essential component.

47 Do you fantasise when making love?

   a Never – there is no need when you have the real thing.

   b Seldom – you don't feel relaxed enough most of the time.

   c Often – it adds spice to an already exciting occasion.

48 You know your partner really loves you when:

   a He/she turns down a chance to do something he/she enjoys to spend an evening with you.

   b You feel a grotty mess and he/she tells you you're beautiful.

   c He/she offers to be your nubile slave and obey your every command.

49 In which historical era would you most like to have lived?

  a Victorian times.
  b The Middle Ages.
  c The Roman Empire.

50 Here are three ways songwriters have described love. Which line from a song applies to you?

  a 'Love is a many splendoured thing; in the morning mist, two lovers kiss, and the world goes zing'.
  b 'One must never deny it, but after you try it, you vary the diet'.
  c 'Love and marriage, go together like a horse and carriage'.

SCORING

Question	Passionate	Playful	Practical
1	a	b	c
2	b	c	a
3	c	b	a
4	b	c	a
5	c	b	a
6	a	b	c
7	c	a	b
8	b	c	a
9	b	c	a
10	c	a	b
11	a	b	c
12	c	b	a
13	a	c	b
14	b	a	c
15	a	b	c
16	b	a	c
17	c	b	a
18	c	a	b
19	b	c	a
20	a	c	b
21	a	b	c
22	b	a	c
23	c	b	a
24	a	b	c

Question	Passionate	Playful	Practical
25	c	a	b
26	a	b	c
27	b	c	a
28	b	a	c
29	b	a	c
30	c	b	a
31	a	b	c
32	b	a	c
33	a	b	c
34	c	b	a
35	a	b	c
36	c	a	b
37	b	c	a
38	a	b	c
39	b	c	a
40	b	c	a
41	a	c	b
42	a	b	c
43	c	a	b
44	b	a	c
45	a	b	c
46	c	a	b
47	a	c	b
48	b	c	a
49	b	c	a
50	a	b	c

Total up the number of answers you have given that fall in each of these columns, giving yourself a score out of 50 on each love style. This will give you an idea of your personal balance among the three primary types of love. Few people are so extreme that they score 50 on one and nothing on the others, but a score of 25 or more on any scale may be considered high.

Most people get on best with others who have similar scores and gross discrepancies may help to explain tensions in your relationship. However, small differences of say 7 or 8 points are not important, and do not forget the characteristic differences between men and women.

17

ARE YOU AND YOUR LOVER
COMPATIBLE?

Like two peas in a pod, or chalk and cheese? Perhaps you have never paused to ponder whether you are ideally suited to your present partner. If so, that is probably a good sign – unless you are unusually submissive and fatalistic. Here is an opportunity to review the quality of your relationship; it may not tell you anything you do not already know somewhere in your heart of hearts, but it may bring the facts home to you with greater than previous clarity.

Over the years, psychologists have evaluated two rival theories as regards partner compatibility. One is the idea that opposites attract, sometimes called *complementation* theory, and the other is expressed by the proverb 'birds of a feather flock together', known technically as *similarity* theory. For the most part, research has supported the latter idea – couples staying together the longest and expressing the greatest happiness tending to be more alike in most respects than couples whose relationships are unstable and unhappy. This applies particularly with respect to attributes such as age, intelligence, attractiveness, social class, education, religion, and social and political attitudes. The political factor is perhaps most obvious. Two people with extreme right and left views respectively are bound to argue about current affairs. Shared hobbies and interests are also predictive of successful relationships, if only because they keep the couple together and give them something to talk about other than routine domestic matters.

As regards personality, similarity still appears preferable to dissimilarity, but it is much less important and the complementation effect seems almost equally viable. For example, if one party likes to do a lot of talking, it is no bad thing that the other is a good listener.

There is another sense in which the complementation hypothesis has proved valid. Where there is a difference between men and women on average in the population, it seems to be optimal if the particular relationship reflects that difference. For example, men are on average about 4 or 5 inches taller than women, and there is evidence that, other things being equal, partnerships are more stable if the man is taller than the woman.

Other attributes which show typical sex differences, and for which the same principle has been found to apply, are dominance versus submission, libido, emotionality and artistic versus scientific/technical interests. In each case, partnerships appear to be more satisfying if the man is traditionally masculine in relation to the woman, and the woman traditionally feminine relative to the man. It remains open to argument as to whether this state of affairs is determined by nature or by the particular social environment that prevails in the world today. We are moving closer to sexual equality, but *identity* is another matter – there will probably always be ways in which men and women complement each other in their attributes.

Finally, we should not forget that a major contribution to compatibility comes from less easily definable and measurable sources that can best be described as the *chemistry* of a relationship. This does not refer simply to body smells and pheromones (although chemistry in this literal sense may also be relevant). It includes a great range of cues that may have emotional significance to us, and very often quite unconsciously – people's gestures, the way they walk, the shape of their nose, the length of their hair, the tone of their voice, and so on. Is there something about them that reminds us of the father we loved, the headmaster we revered, the kindly aunt who played with us as a child? There is some evidence to support the Freudian idea that when we fall in love in adulthood, we are within certain limits replacing the opposite sex parent to whom we became attached in infancy. At the very least, our experience of our parents, and attitude towards them, appears to be an important factor in our choice of a partner.

These mysterious factors, which we lump together under the term 'chemistry', are more difficult to address in a questionnaire than more easily reported attributes, such as education and food preferences, but they nevertheless appear indirectly in that good feelings and irritations are seldom merely what they seem – they are motivated in many complex ways, including the unconscious dynamics described above.

To check your compatibility with your lover, answer the questions below – but not with your partner looking over your shoulder, and not unless you are prepared to discover (or be reminded of) the worst. Later on, you might want to take the risk of having your lover do the quiz so that you can compare your answers. Choose one answer only for each question.

1   GENERAL RELATIONSHIP

1   Do you often think about ending your relationship?

   a It would be very painful if you were to part.
   b When you are fed up with your partner.
   c It is almost a daily occurrence.

2   How much do you and your partner confide in each other?

   a You tell each other all your most intimate fears and fantasies.
   b There are some things in your lives you would prefer to keep private.
   c The survival of your relationship depends on regular deception.

3   On your birthday, your partner would:

   a Instinctively know exactly what would please you.
   b Probably buy you something you have to exchange later.
   c Manage to waste money on a totally unsuitable gift.

4   Do you like to be alone together?

   a Your partner is the most stimulating person you know.
   b You feel that a break from each other enhances your appreciation.
   c You try to reduce the boredom by surrounding yourself with acquaintances.

5   What sort of arguments do you have?

   a Disagreements are openly aired and quickly resolved.
   b There are some topics which you had better avoid discussing.
   c You constantly bicker, on trivia as well as major issues.

6   Have you made a good choice in your partner?

   a You have never met anyone who made you feel quite so fulfilled.
   b You believe life is a compromise and you are reasonably well-suited.
   c You are making the best of a bad job and biding time in the hope that someone better will turn up.

7 You arrive home hot and tired from work. Your partner would:

   a Make allowances for your bad temper and do his/her best to put you in a good humour.

   b Pour you a stiff drink and stay out of your way for a while.

   c Regale you with problems of his/her own before you could sit down.

8 When you go to a party, you are always on the lookout for:

   a Stimulating conversation.

   b New friendships.

   c A replacement for your partner.

9 You find your partner in a passionate clinch with a very attractive person. Your concern is for:

   a Your apparent inability to satisfy them.

   b Your lost youth.

   c Losing your financial security.

10 Overall, how would you describe your relationship?

   a The perfect love match.

   b Passionate, but with definite ups and downs.

   c Slightly better than complete loneliness.

2 DEMOGRAPHIC FACTORS

1 How does your height compare with that of your partner?

   a The man is taller than the woman.

   b You are around the same height.

   c The woman is taller than the man.

2 How does your weight compare?

   a Fat or thin, you are similar in shape.

   b The man is somewhat overweight.

   c The woman is much heavier than the man.

3 Is there a gap in your ages?

   a There are only a few years between you.

   b The man is considerably older than the woman.

   c The woman is considerably older than the man.

4   How do people rate you and your lover in looks?

    a You are considered similar in attractiveness.

    b Your lover is better looking in a conventional way, but you also have admirers.

    c Your lover is plain compared to yourself.

5   What occupations are you in?

    a You both have interesting jobs with a lot in common to discuss.

    b You have rewarding but very different occupations.

    c One stays home while the other partner has an exciting career.

6   Are you a healthy person?

    a Generally speaking, you enjoy excellent health.

    b You are prone to colds but seldom get anything serious.

    c You catch anything going around.

7   People observing your body language would find you and your partner:

    a In perfect synchrony.

    b Largely in tune with each other.

    c In direct opposition.

8   How do you compare with regard to social class?

    a Pretty much the same.

    b Some discrepancy, but you are little affected.

    c You are often aware of a gap in social background.

9   Is your educational background similar?

    a You attended similar institutions and achieved much the same level.

    b You attended different types of school, but reached a similar level.

    c You are like chalk and cheese.

10   Were you born in the same country as your partner?

    a Yes.

    b No, but you currently agree on where you want to live.

    c No, and you disagree about where it is best to live.

3 SEXUAL COMPATIBILITY

1 Do you have similar views on pornography?

 a You are in absolute agreement.
 b Your partner is perhaps a little more (or less) liberal than you.
 c You are strongly opposed to your partner's viewpoint.

2 In bed with your lover you feel:

 a Stimulated.
 b Content.
 c Bored.

3 Does your lover know precisely how to give you sexual pleasure?

 a You feel totally satisfied after love-making.
 b You are shy of telling him/her what turns you on most.
 c You can't count the times they go off to sleep leaving you frustrated.

4 Your partner brings home a tape describing techniques of erotic massage. You:

 a Can't wait to try it out on each other.
 b Take a bath and wait for a demonstration.
 c Think it commercialises sex.

5 Are there aspects of personal hygiene which concern you about your lover?

 a None at all, he/she is very fastidious.
 b He/she doesn't always wash him/herself as thoroughly as you'd like.
 c Some of his/her habits appal you.

6 Your lover prefers sex in a position that causes you some discomfort. Do you:

 a Tell him/her and try new ways of giving him/her satisfaction.
 b Suffer in silence, prepared to put up with a little pain to make him/her happy.
 c Stop love-making and feign tiredness when he/she suggests it.

7 How do you rate the importance of fidelity?

   a You and your partner have similar views.
   b It can be a matter of debate and disagreement.
   c Your values on this issue are diametrically opposed.

8 What do you think about contraception?

   a You and your lover are of like mind.
   b There is some dispute as regards method.
   c You cannot agree as to whether it should be used at all.

9 How does your sex drive compare with that of your partner?

   a You enjoy sex equally.
   b You sometimes find your partner too demanding or
      uninterested sexually.
   c You never feel like making love at the same time.

10 How far would you be prepared to go to please your partner
      sexually?

   a You would happily succumb to his/her desires, knowing that
      anything he/she enjoys would please you too.
   b As long as he/she would 'meet you halfway' on your
      enjoyment, you would go along with his/her wishes.
   c It is of greater concern to you that your partner finds ways to
      satisfy you.

4 ATTITUDES AND INTERESTS

1 On an evening out, do you easily agree on where to eat?

   a You both like the same food and have favourite restaurants.
   b You have some preferences which are not shared by your
      partner.
   c You dislike just about every restaurant your partner
      suggests.

2 To what extent do you share political views?

   a You are often surprised at how close you are in ideology.
   b There are certain political points on which you could not
      agree.
   c As far as you are concerned, your partner is a dreamer when
      it comes to politics.

3 Do cultural differences in your background impose a strain on your relationship?

   a You both respect the other's cultural background and delight in broadening your cultural horizons through your partner.

   b Cultural differences occasionally make you feel a distinct lack of communication.

   c You are certain your partner's background is to blame for his/her peculiar behaviour.

4 Can you agree on how to raise children?

   a Your love for each other will easily extend to your offspring.

   b You can each more or less tolerate the other's ideals.

   c You think it best not to have any children since you could see their upbringing would cause major rifts between you.

5 Is religion a problem in your relationship?

   a Not at all – you both have the same religious beliefs.

   b There are some differences, but you agree to disagree.

   c Your religious differences cause major upsets.

6 Do you disagree on the handling of money?

   a You always agree on how to allocate your budget.

   b You have occasional tiffs on money matters.

   c You find your partner overly mean or extravagant.

7 If your lover asked you to an art gallery or poetry reading, you would:

   a Eagerly anticipate the event.

   b Go with some reservations.

   c Suggest he/she goes alone.

8 What do you think about your partner's taste in clothes?

   a He/she dresses with impeccable taste and usually to please you.

   b Most of the time he/she is a credit to you.

   c You are sometimes so ashamed of the way he/she is turned out, you pretend to be with someone else.

9 How do you feel about your partner's friends?

   a Great fun and your kind of people.

   b Some of his/her friends leave you cold.

   c You prefer to see your own friends.

10 How do you think the male and female roles should be divided?

   a You take life as it comes and find it unnecessary to allocate specific tasks according to gender.
   b You have an understanding between you as to who should take responsibility for what.
   c Your partner appears to be living in the 'Middle Ages' – so blinkered is his/her thinking in these matters.

5   PERSONALITY

1 How well are you suited temperamentally?

   a You really enjoy your partner's personality.
   b Although you have different temperaments, you tend to complement each other.
   c You are poles apart in temperament.

2 Do you have a high regard for your partner's intellect?

   a He/she never ceases to amaze you with his/her wide knowledge and insight.
   b While his/her intelligence may not be on a par with your own, he/she compensates with other attributes.
   c A 'great mind' is not a particular feature in your partner.

3 What irritates you most about your partner?

   a You recognise faults in him/her which you have yourself.
   b His/her quick temper.
   c His/her disgusting habits.

4 Is a shared sense of humour an important basis of your friendship?

   a You are always having a good laugh together.
   b There are times when your partner's sense of humour eludes you.
   c You seldom find the same things funny.

5 Do you like to travel?

   a Yes – you both enjoy new experiences.
   b You are both content with the home environment.

   c One of you is an intrepid voyager and the other likes to stay at home.

6 Is your relationship marred by temper outbursts?

   a No – you are both very easy going.
   b You sometimes have to bottle up grievances.
   c Rows are both common and bitter.

7 Is either of you inclined to depressive episodes?

   a No – you are both generally cheerful and optimistic.
   b If one of you 'has the hump', the other can usually lift him/her out of it.
   c You have a depressing effect on each other.

8 Is there a clear pecking order between you?

   a Yes, but each recognises the other's superiority in certain fields.
   b One of you is dominant in every respect.
   c There is a perpetual struggle for power between you.

9 How adventurous are you?

   a About the same degree.
   b The man is more exploratory than the woman.
   c The woman is sensation seeking while the man is inhibited.

10 Are you troubled by fears and anxieties?

   a Not really – you are both fairly stable.
   b One is prone to worry about things but the other has a calming influence.
   c You are both on the verge of a nervous breakdown.

SCORING

The quiz deals with five different, though overlapping, areas of compatibility and incompatibility. For each section, add up the number of 'a', 'b' and 'c' answers that you gave. Give yourself 1 point for each 'c' answer, 2 points for each 'b' and 3 points for each 'a'.

   You should now have five scores, representing totals for each section that will be somewhere in the range of 10–30.

1   General Relationship

This section concerns the quality of your interpersonal relationship with your partner – how much you like to be together, how much intimacy and caring there is, how you deal with disagreements, jealousies, etc – and the whole process of give and take. In many ways, this is the most sensitive indicator of compatibility since it affects, and is influenced by, all the other more specific areas.

A score of 25 or over indicates a very high level of compatibility and 20–24 is a very reasonable average. 15–19 suggests some degree of discontent, while 10–14 is indicative of a rather sorry state.

2   Demographic factors

This group of items concerns such matters as age, height and occupation – the sort of things that insurance companies use to base predictions of risk. Ideally, these should not matter in a marriage or relationship, but research and experience tell us that they do. To a degree, differences may add spice to a relationship, but if they are too many and too striking, they may lead to incompatibility in the long term.

The same scale applies as above: 25 or over, you are highly compatible; 20–24, satisfactory; 15–19, cause for concern; 10–14, unstable.

3   Sexual compatibility

These questions deal with various aspects of your sex life. It may be possible for you to have a good relationship with a very low level of sexual activity if this is what suits you both, but difficulties arise when there is a great gulf between you as regards sexual attitudes, appetite and preferences.

As above, you may assess your sexual compatibility according to the following scale: 25 or over, excellent; 20–24 satisfactory; 15–19 below average; 10–14 unsatisfactory. If sex is your only, or major, focus of incompatibility, you might consider whether sex therapy might have something to offer you.

4   Attitudes and interests

This factor deals with matters of ideology, taste, preferences and general philosophy of life which are known to be important determinants of long-term compatibility. Again, people do not have to be identical in order to live happily together, but a certain amount of common ground is necessary and the more shared viewpoints the better. Use the same scale as before to assess your compatibility in this area.

5 Personality

The last section of the quiz focuses on personality predispositions and temperament. As noted previously, not all differences in personality are detrimental, some may even enhance a relationship by a process of complementation. Nevertheless, there are several ways in which two personalities may clash and produce unhappiness and the questions here have been chosen to tap these sources of strain in a relationship. The same scoring key applies as for the previous sections.

Overall compatibility

Now that you have looked at your compatibility rating in the five different areas, you may like to consider it overall by adding your five scores together. This will give you a total score of between 50 and 150, which may be understood as follows:

Score: 130–150

You are exceptionally lucky to have such a good relationship. Your future as a couple looks destined to be long and happy.

Score: 110–129

Your relationship is fairly rewarding and you should be able to maintain a long-term happy association. A little more tolerance and consideration on your own part could do nothing but good. Remember that true love consists of a willingness to give with no expectation of direct return.

Score: 90–109

Your relationship is average enough but with definite signs of discontent. If you are not yet married, you should think long and hard before committing yourself further. If you are already married, you might ask yourself whether your relationship could be improved with a little more effort and unselfishness. You might also consider marriage guidance, perhaps taking your answers to these questions along with you for discussion.

Score: 50—89

If you are not yet committed to this person you would be well advised not to become further involved. If already married, you are perhaps staying together for the sake of the children, economics, convenience or some other external constraint. Ask yourself seriously whether you might not be happier living apart and talk it over with a marriage counsellor.

18

HOW GOOD A LOVER ARE YOU?

What does it take to make a great lover? Is it the ability to seduce countless women, like Don Juan or Casanova? Is it mysterious, exotic passion like Rudolph Valentino as 'The Sheik'? Is it willingness to sacrifice all, including one's life, in favour of the loved one, like Juliet or Isolde? Some may think in such grandiose and melodramatic terms, but for most of us what is important is the ability to make one special person happy and contented by the way that we treat him/her – not just sexually, but in all areas of life.

For all the pining and acts of self-destruction that are performed by the great romantic lovers of literature, most of them lived lives that were remote from the object of their affection. Seldom did they get to know each other really well, from direct experience of day-to-day living. They were as much in love with a fantasy, or the idea of love itself, as they were with a real person. If they had been required to spend more time together and share the dull routine of domestic existence, worrying about the children's earache and how to afford the roof repairs, their relationship might have seemed less idyllic. The love of ordinary people is at the same time more difficult and more real.

Being a good lover does include a certain amount of seductiveness. Men like Casanova usually know a great deal about self-presentation and the sort of attention that makes a woman feel good. The trouble is that they use these skills to manipulate women for their own selfish, lustful ends – to coin a phrase, their only interest is 'to have their way with them'. The art of history's great seducers may nevertheless be studied with advantage by men who wish to make a favourable impression and maintain the interest of their regular partner.

For both men and women, it is important to continue looking and smelling good, and generally to make oneself attractive to the partner, no matter how secure one feels in the relationship. Going steady or being married does not give us licence to relax all standards of grooming, dress or hygiene.

It is also important for both men and women to realise that a partner is bound to get slightly bored if they always have to make the running sexually. Sometimes it is relaxing to be a passive recipient of sexual advances – even a 'victim' of someone else's desires. Many women fear that their man would feel threatened or disgusted if on occasion they took it upon themselves to call the tune and play the role of the sexual aggressor. Such men do exist, but they are very much in a minority; for most men, fantasy women are markedly more assertive and adventurous in bed than real women.

Another thing that Casanova knew well and that any lover might profit by learning (if they have not already done so) is the importance of attentiveness. This means showing that you think about the other person, for example by listening to his/her conversation and remembering what he/she says, and, more obviously, by presenting little gifts and compliments, especially when they will be a surprise and not part of an occasion such as a birthday, or an apology for a misdeed. Again, this applies equally to men and women.

The important thing about a gift is not so much what it cost but the thought behind it. An inexpensive gift that is appropriate in some way to the receiver is much more appreciated than a costly one which might just as well have been purchased for someone else. It is gratifying to the lover to see that you have thought in advance what he/she might especially like or seen something in a store that immediately reminded you of him/her. Personal, intimate items, such as underwear or cologne, are especially appropriate gifts between lovers, and 'luxury' items, such as flowers or jewellery, are generally better appreciated than functional items, such as brooms and bottle openers. The fact that a gift appears for no good reason makes it particularly welcome and memorable.

Ideally, a compliment is unsolicited by requests such as 'How do you like my new tie?' or 'What do you think of my latest painting?' But most important is that the compliment is true, or at least heartfelt, for only then is it likely to be credible. It is counterproductive to say 'What beautiful skin you have' to a person with terminal acne, or 'What a manly frame you have' to the kind of scrawny wimp that everyone kicks sand in the face of at the beach. Lying about virtues that a person does not possess is called flattery, and it is seldom convincing in the long term. To make an effective compliment it is best to think of something about your lover that you really *do* like and comment upon that. This has the useful side-effect of reminding you what it is about them that you appreciate, and perhaps why you fell in love with them in the first place.

Another way of showing that you love a person is to do things for him/her that he/she likes. This may range from making him/her a cup of coffee in the morning or a special meal in the evening, repairing a piece of electrical equipment, mowing their lawn, driving him/her somewhere – in fact, displaying a skill or filling a role that is in some way different or complementary to his/her own. Providing somebody with a special expertise or service that does not come easily to him/her is a good way to his/her heart. This is, after all, partly why he/she 'needs' you.

The same principle applies in sexual love-making. The skilled lover is sensitive to the needs of the other, is always learning more about them, and concentrates on giving pleasure rather than receiving it. All the peripheral things and preambles, such as kissing, stroking, caressing, massaging, verbal compliments, encouragement and simple expressions of love are just as important as a virtuoso, gymnastic performance in the act of intercourse itself – and probably more so. The 'overture' and 'exit music' are just as important as the show itself when a couple make love.

It is important to remember that you do not own your partner. However much they say they belong to you, you should never feel you have the right to treat them as property. They must maintain some degree of independence and privacy and they will need to have contact with people other than yourself, including members of the opposite sex. To feel jealousy when your partner is attracted to someone else (as they are almost certain to be from time to time) is perfectly natural, but that does not justify an indignant, self-righteous, angry outburst. Manifest jealousy is seldom a pretty emotion; it is usually seen as selfish and immature and is almost invariably counterproductive.

Finally, do not expect your lover to be what he/she is not. People cannot easily change. Love them for what they actually are or you might just as well move on to find someone more suitable. And do not demand that they love you better, or even, force them to *say* that they love you. Love, and the expression of it, is spontaneously given, or it is not sincere. And if it is not sincere, it is worthless.

I What is a good lover? A person who:

   a Sacrifices his/her personality and feeling for his/her lover.
   b Will lay down his/her life for love.
   c Makes the world a happy and beautiful place for his/her lover.

2 How often must you have sex to be a good lover?

   a Twice a week.
   b When your lover wants it.
   c When you desire each other.

3 You know your lover appreciates you when:

   a He/she accepts expensive presents from you.
   b He/she is prepared to kill to protect your honour.
   c He/she loves you despite your faults.

4 Your partner fancies someone of the opposite sex. You:

   a Beg them not to be unfaithful.
   b Vow to destroy your rival.
   c Would find it strange if they fancied no-one but you.

5 The words 'I love you' should be told to you:

   a When you ask your lover.
   b Every time you speak to each other.
   c When they are spontaneous and genuine.

6 After living together you find there are some things you can't stand about your lover. You:

   a Are determined to bring him/her round to your way of thinking.
   b Hate imperfections in people and would prefer to end your relationship.
   c Accept that we are all different and concentrate on enjoying his/her good points.

7 What gift would you buy a lover, given a large budget?

   a A new car.
   b A priceless jewel.
   c Something small that was of particular and exclusive value to him/her.

8 What is the best recipe for long-term success in a relationship?

   a Secure financial ties.
   b Devoted, undying love.
   c Friendship, trust and deep affection.

9 Introducing your lover to a social set he/she is unfamiliar with, the first thing you establish is:

   a Registering with everyone to whom they belong.
   b Finding a secluded corner you can rush off to when he/she has met a few people.
   c Effecting an introduction to the most interesting and amusing people in the group.

10 What effect would children have on you and your lover?

   a Children would hold your relationship together.
   b Children would interfere with your idyllic state.
   c Children would be facsimilies of you and your lover and a constant reminder of each other.

11 The way to satisfy your lover is to:

   a Perform like a sexual athlete.
   b Consume him/her with passion.
   c Discover precisely what thrills him/her.

12 How often do you titivate yourself with creams and fragrances?

   a When time or the occasion permits.
   b When you are meeting your lover.
   c You take care of your body with a regular grooming routine.

13 Would you dress up specially for your lover?

   a You don't have to impress him/her any more.
   b You dress exclusively for your lover.
   c You especially enjoy turning him/her on by wearing something exciting when you make love.

14 Are you fastidious about personal hygiene?

   a Only dirty people need to bathe daily.
   b You will only bathe with your lover.
   c Hygiene is an essential part of love-making.

15 Which statement do you agree with:

   a It's up to a man to call the tune sexually.
   b A man would be robbed of his masculinity if the woman is aggressive.
   c Most men adore being taken by an adventurous and sexually assertive woman.

16 Could you tell better than most people what your lover is thinking?

   a How can you possibly know if he/she doesn't tell you.

   b You share some mystical telepathy with your lover.

   c You are so completely in tune you know instinctively what he/she desires.

17 Are you complimentary to your lover on his/her achievements?

   a You always flatter him/her falsely to hold his/her attention.

   b Everything your lover does is 'God-like' and you praise him/her lavishly.

   c You respond with warmth and admiration when he/she achieves something deserving.

18 If your lover has a problem he/she would:

   a Sort it out for him/herself.

   b Not want to bother you with it.

   c Discuss it at length with you.

19 Your lover enjoys a particular kind of food that you don't. You:

   a Suggest that he/she buys it if he/she wants it.

   b Force yourself to enjoy it too.

   c Keep a constant supply in the fridge for him/her.

20 Could you remember the last conversation you had with your partner?

   a You forget – he/she was prattling on about something or other.

   b You cling to his/her every syllable.

   c Your conversations are always of interest to you both.

21 You are ready to go out on a date and your lover arrives to collect you – weary from overwork. You:

   a Get angry and suggest you go without him/her.

   b Stay home to appease his/her every need.

   c Offer him/her a hot bath and massage to relax before you go out.

22 How much do you have to learn about your lover?

   a You know all there is to know about the opposite sex.

   b You await his/her every move with bated breath.

   c You discover new facets of his/her personality every day.

23 Does your lover trust you completely in sex?

  a He/she gets pretty sensitive for fear you might handle his/her genitals roughly.

  b His/her faith in you is blinding and implicit.

  c He/she willingly abandons him/herself to your exploring fingers.

24 What is your ultimate goal when you make love?

  a To obtain maximum satisfaction for yourself.

  b To enter into a spiritual orbit together.

  c To make each time fantastic and memorable for your lover.

25 Imagine your lover is bedridden but feeling sexy. You would:

  a Put something in his/her tea to kill the desire.

  b Can't bear to see them incapacitated and prefer to go away until he/she recovers.

  c Look for new ways to give them sexual fulfilment.

26 Do you have any major disagreements on what you do in bed?

  a You can't pluck up enough courage to tell him/her that you don't like a lot of things he/she does.

  b You never discuss it – love-making is an aesthetic, ethereal experience.

  c Nothing you do sexually has ever caused dissension between you.

27 Do you go out of your way to create imaginative scenarios for your lover?

  a Sounds like a pretty infantile way to behave – straight sex is fine for you.

  b You only see them in exotic far-away places.

  c Yes, the mind is probably the most powerful aphrodisiac of all.

28 Have you ever whispered to your lover when you are out together that you are not wearing any underwear to excite him/her?

  a You wouldn't dare – supposing you got run over by a bus . . .?

  b No – you are usually wearing nothing prior to love-making.

  c Yes – you adore to tease him/her.

29 A candle-lit dinner together would be:

a A good way to hide physical imperfections.
b The only way to dine.
c An opportunity for sexy talk and a build-up to love-making.

30 After a night of passionate love-making, the first thing you do in the morning is:

a Tell your lover to fetch breakfast since you gave them such a good time.
b Draw the curtains and drift back to sleep in his/her arms.
c Get your lover some coffee and slip back into bed with him/her.

31 Your lover complains of a headache. You:

a Tell him/her where to find the aspirin.
b Could not conceive of him/her suffering in your company.
c Ease the pain with deft finger-work on his/her forehead and nape of neck.

32 Circumstances force you apart for several weeks. You:

a Are pleased to have a break to sort out your life.
b Pine away and cannot eat.
c Keep in touch with funny anecdotes and sexy stories.

33 Top of your list of priorities after a long separation is:

a Sorting out domestic problems.
b Re-affirmation of your lover's devotion to you.
c An urgent desire to make love.

34 A long holiday together would result in an overall feeling of:

a Boredom and loneliness.
b Sublime togetherness.
c Lust and sexual fulfilment.

35 Your lover starts filling the house with erotic paintings and statues. You:

a Refuse to put them on show in case the neighbours see them.
b Are impressed by anything he/she does or says.
c Take delight in finding new objects to add to the collection.

36 Naked in bed beside your lover, you would:

  a Pull up the bedclothes so you don't freeze.
  b Lie cradled in his/her arms and drift off to heaven.
  c Stroke and caress him/her all over with your hands, lips and body.

37 Your lover asks you to relate a fantasy to them while you are making love. You:

  a Are not very inventive and prefer to concentrate on what you are doing.
  b Do not need fantasy to interrupt your perfect love.
  c Willingly oblige, knowing what a stimulating effect it has on him/her.

38 Do you use special terms of endearment when you want to be nice to each other?

  a You call each other by your given names, or else nothing.
  b You have a special mystical name for each other.
  c You address your lover by a number of pet names that are very affectionate.

39 How long can a sexual relationship realistically last?

  a Once you have exhausted all the physical possibilities, familiarity and boredom set in.
  b As long as you have each other.
  c The more you find out about a lover, the easier it becomes to excite him/her.

40 Do you genuinely enjoy love-making?

  a Only occasionally, you mostly do it because it is expected of you.
  b The act itself serves to engulf you and your lover into one being.
  c Making love is one of life's greatest pleasures.

SCORING

Add up the number of 'a', 'b' and 'c' responses that you gave separately, to arrive at three scores out of 40. Note which category you scored highest on and interpret your performance as follows:

Mostly 'a's

It seems that you are somewhat lacking in skill as a lover. Either that, or the particular relationship that you have at the moment is so stale and unrewarding that you are not sufficiently motivated to turn in your best performance. One way or another, it is hard to imagine that you or your partner are getting much genuine satisfaction out of being together.

Then again, perhaps you do not have a partner at the moment, or find it generally difficult to attract the opposite sex. If that is the case, then it has to be said that this is not entirely surprising, for your approach and attitude to love-making is not one that would endear you to many people in the long term.

The main problem is that you seem excessively wrapped up in yourself, your own security and satisfaction. You are so intent on receiving what you think is due to you that you lack the capacity to give of yourself – warmth and affection being more important than material contributions.

You also appear rather inhibited and worried about what other people might think. You are more concerned about impressing the world at large than those closest to you. Often, you seem to take the attitude that you can coast along in your relationship on the basis of some kind of imagined credit that you have built up in the past, or take your lover for granted because he/she is committed to you by bonds of social pressure, habit, economic necessity or suchlike. If so, you might one day receive a nasty shock, perhaps returning to an empty house and a farewell note.

If you have a relationship that you wish to preserve, think well about your behaviour and how rewarding you would be to live with. Put yourself in your lover's position for a moment and ask yourself how you would feel. If you are anxious about your lack of success in the mating game, ask yourself the equivalent question – how would you react to a lover who behaved like yourself.

Mostly 'b's

To all intents and purposes you would appear to be the perfect lover – approaching love-making with unswerving dedication and devotion. Unfortunately, your rather extreme behaviour is based on a somewhat naïve perception of human beings.

It is possible that you have just fallen in love, and are wrapped up with the idea of being in love, more than the reality of whom you are loving. Or perhaps your rather melodramatic idealism is a result of reading too many romantic novels. You appear to have lost sight of the fact that even the great lovers of history had 'off days'. Your desire for an exclusive 'life or death' relationship with your lover will eventually become stifling and oppressive to him/her, and your romantic dream could overnight become a nightmare from which he/she will want to escape.

It does not seem likely that anyone could bear the demands you would make on them, so could it be that you do not have a current lover and are fantasising about your concept of a perfect love?

In fact, you have many attributes which are admirable – unselfishness and a generous heart. If you can adjust your perspective and tone down some of your ideals, you could make your lover a very happy person.

Try to come to terms with human frailties and prepare to accept others' faults. Nobody can take being elevated on a pedestal for the rest of his/her life; if he/she does not come crashing down in your eyes at some point in time, he/she is bound to take a suicidal leap. With your passionate nature and with so much to give, all that is necessary is for you to learn to love more honestly and realistically and you and your lover are set to enjoy a very fulfilling relationship.

Mostly 'c's

Your lover, if you have one, is a very fortunate person. Your love is realistic and practical, besides being warm and supportive. You have the skill and willingness to provide him/her with sexual stimulation and companionship based on a true perception of his/her personality and needs rather than looking past him/her as a person to some ideal concept that has no reality except in your imagination. Your rose-coloured spectacles may have been shattered at some time, or been deliberately discarded by you, but still you manage to give warmth, affection and friendship to your partner.

If you are currently without a partner, it would be surprising, and it can hardly be put down to your deficiency in social skills. You have a great deal to offer and it is only a matter of time before somebody will want to enjoy a relationship with you. Perhaps you think you are better off without any attachment or commitment, but more likely not. You are a born lover and will find your deepest fulfilment in exercising your skill.

Mixture of 'a's, 'b's and 'c's

Of course, few people will have consistently opted for one scoring category. Probably, the comments made above all apply to you to some extent. Look at the balance of the three scores in order to find out to what extent you should take the advice as being directed at you personally.

Finally, feel free to reject the advice given if, without ego-defensiveness, you genuinely disagree with it. Other people can call things the way they see them, and offer suggestions but, ultimately, your relationship with another person is your own responsibility and nobody's business but your own.

19

HOW GOOD IS YOUR LOVER?

Now that you have found out how good you are as a lover, you may like to make a similar assessment of your partner. In doing so, of course, you will not be able to arrive at any conclusions concerning his/her prowess in general terms; it is virtually impossible for you to know how good a lover he/she might be with someone else – with past, future, or dare we say, current, other lovers. He/she may be a paragon of romance and a sexual dynamo with other people, but an absolute pig to you. It must be appreciated from the outset, that this quiz will only tell you how good a lover your partner is to *you personally*. But no matter – from your point of view that is what really counts.

Many marriage counsellors or sex therapists, seeing a couple jointly, have had to contend with complaints from the wife that her husband is impotent, while on the side, he admits to stud-like prowess with his pretty young secretary. Similarly, there are plenty of wives who are 'frigid' where their husband is concerned, but readily aroused by the milkman or next-door neighbour. But in cases such as these, it is usually possible to detect something fundamentally wrong with the relationship as a whole.

It is unlikely that you will discover anything radically surprising as a result of completing the quiz that follows. Most of us are aware, at some level of consciousness, of the strengths and deficiencies of our relationships. Nevertheless, it may be illuminating to work through a systematic series of questions and arrive at a quantified index of how well our partner behaves towards us. It may be no more or less than we deserve, but still it is interesting to find out.

LOVERS' ETIQUETTE

First, it may be instructive to ask how an ideal lover ought, and ought not, to behave. The cardinal rule, under which most others may be incorporated, is that he/she should be considerate of your feelings. He/she should strive at all times to see things from your point of view and to be warm and supportive as far as possible. In other words, he/she should try, and usually succeed, to make you feel good.

This does not mean they are obliged to be a doormat at all times and give in to your every whim. A mature relationship is one in which your ideas, needs and feelings are expressed reciprocally and taken into consideration before any course of action is embarked upon. The important thing is that each partner understands the other's point of view before the give and take is negotiated; that way any disputes remain superficial.

It may be that your lover (and you for that matter) cannot help being attracted to other people. If this is inevitable, it does not necessarily have to be destructive – it all depends how tolerant you each are in this department and how things are handled. The most unforgivable sin is to humiliate your partner publicly, by deserting, insulting, or otherwise maltreating and belittling them in pursuit of other people. If your partner forgets that you exist and have feelings whenever another attractive person appears over the horizon then you have definite cause for dissatisfaction.

Regardless of whether one is showing off to an attractive person, it is bad form to criticise a partner in front of other people. How often have you seen a couple, usually long established together, who delight in telling friends, relatives and even complete strangers all about the little habits, foibles, mistakes and inadequacies of the other? Apart from the fact that this practice is somewhat obscene and that nobody else really wants to hear about these things, it only exposes one's own ego problems and is intensely embarrassing and irritating to the partner.

Nor is it necessary to do the exact opposite – to fondle the partner in public, call him/her by cutesy, babyish names, and carry on about how good he/she is to you and what a wonderful, talented person he/she is. This is likely to be seen from the outside as protesting too much (trying to persuade oneself, along with the rest of the world), and it is likely eventually to irritate the partner as well. A good lover is neither heavily critical and destructive nor effusively over-affectionate in front of others.

When in private, the rule of consideration to the other applies with equal force. The ideal lover is sensitive to your moods, and does not push sexual advances harder or faster than they can be received with a similar amount of pleasure. This can present a problem when one partner has a much greater need for sex than the other – a break-up is probable in the absence of radical adaptations. In a recent book, a middle-aged professional man described how he was converted to the yogi ideal of celibacy by being made by his wife to feel either like a rapist or a beggar when he approached her for sex. But given some kind of balance of libido, there are bound to be times when one partner feels sexier than the other and must take account of the other's slower arousal.

Other rules for the etiquette of lovers were given in connection with the previous quiz. Jealousy may be felt, and even expressed, but not viciously and self-righteously. Gifts should be intimate and personal and sometimes spontaneous and unexpected – not just reserved for ritual occasions or apologies. Expressions of love should be given freely and never required to be produced on demand, or else they are reduced to meaningless formalities. Perhaps, above all, it is important to maintain a sense of humour, of levity, of fun.

There is more than one way in which your partner can make him/herself unpleasant and prove to be a bad lover; the formula for a good lover is more singular, more circumscribed. But enough of preamble, at this stage you may like to answer the questions below to find out whether you are the privileged partner of a dream lover or the victim of a bumbling inadequate.

I You have to leave town, and your lover, to go abroad on business. You spend your time:

    a Preoccupied with worrying whether he/she is being faithful to you.

    b Looking out for someone to have a fling with, pretty sure that your lover will be doing likewise.

    c Getting on with the job in hand while looking forward to his/her telephone call every evening.

2 Would you describe your lover as having sex appeal?

    a Not really, more like a nice person.

    b A bit too much for your liking.

    c It was their animal sexuality which attracted you in the first place.

3 How well do you communicate with your lover?

   a You like to be one jump ahead of him/her since he/she can be a pretty tricky customer.

   b He/she never tells you anything important and only seems interested in going to bed.

   c You are totally in tune to the point where he/she can anticipate your next move.

4 Your favourite TV programme is on at the same time each week as a soap your lover wants to watch on another channel. He/she:

   a Arbitrarily switches on to his/her favourite programme.

   b Retires to another room and watches another set.

   c Is prepared to watch the programme you like.

5 You are not in the mood for sex. Your lover:

   a Tells you that you are frigid/impotent.

   b Threatens to run off with a sexier person.

   c Holds it over till you feel like it too.

6 When you go out together, your partner makes you feel:

   a Like an expensive appendage.

   b Like last year's model.

   c Like the most desirable person in the room.

7 Alone with your lover, what do you tend to do?

   a Your own things.

   b Make love.

   c Share your secrets in bed.

8 Friends who know you as a couple would say your lover was:

   a Disinterested in you.

   b Likely to run off at any time.

   c Exclusively devoted to you.

9 Introducing your lover to your parents, you want him/her to look good. You would:

   a Pretend he/she was dressed badly because he/she had just been gardening.

   b Go out and buy him/her a new outfit to wear.

   c Feel confident he/she would make a good impression.

10 If you have a row, who makes the first move to make up?

   a You have to, as he/she is very stubborn.
   b You can both go for days without speaking.
   c Usually the one who started the row.

11 You both want to see a show with a 'big name' star. Your lover:

   a Expects you to queue in the rain for several hours to get tickets.
   b Bumps into you in the foyer with another date.
   c Magically produces two tickets as a treat for you.

12 Your lover writes you a letter from abroad. It is:

   a Typed on a word-processor.
   b On an airletter to keep the cost down.
   c Sealed with a loving kiss (SWALK).

13 A play you get free tickets to turns out to be a monumental bore. Your lover:

   a Passes loud, rude remarks which make you cringe.
   b Is too busy caressing you to notice.
   c Suggests you slip off to the pub together in the interval and you end up spending the rest of the evening there.

14 When you are feeling unwell, your lover:

   a Tells you to stop being a hypochondriac.
   b Suggests you go to bed and then goes out.
   c Makes a fuss of you and tries to make you better.

15 You give up your weekend to watch your lover enjoy his/her hobby. He/she:

   a Is too busy expecting your praise to notice your sacrifice.
   b Makes you jealous by flirting with other people constantly.
   c Is appreciative of your efforts and proudly shows you off to his/her other friends.

16 When people are talking about your lover you are:

   a Afraid to listen because it's not likely to be complimentary.
   b Suspicious and eager to know if he/she has been having an affair with someone else.
   c Pleased and grateful to know such a popular person.

17 What would your lover list as most important?

   a His/her career success.

   b His/her success with the opposite sex.

   c Making you happy.

18 In bed, does your lover take trouble over the way he/she presents him/herself?

   a He/she expects you to be grateful he/she is with you at all.

   b He/she likes sex that is raw and natural and doesn't bother much with grooming.

   c He/she always makes him/herself clean and nice smelling for you.

19 Does your lover usually keep promises he/she makes to you?

   a No, he/she constantly disappoints you.

   b Only if his/her own pleasure is also involved.

   c You trust his/her word completely – he/she never lets you down.

20 At a party, how does your lover behave towards you?

   a Makes critical comments about the way you conduct yourself.

   b Pursues other attractive guests and expects you to fend for yourself.

   c Ensures you are having a good time, paying special attention whenever you are looking left out.

21 When you go on holiday, who chooses the place?

   a You always leave those decisions to your partner.

   b You both want to go where there are plenty of opportunities to meet the opposite sex.

   c You enjoy the process of looking at brochures and choosing the destination together.

22 What is your lover like when it comes to giving?

   a Rather selfish – only giving you something if he/she knows it is to his/her advantage.

   b If you really needed something you would ask for it, and possibly get it.

   c He/she is spontaneously generous by nature.

23 Do you laugh a lot together?

    a His/her humour is not to your taste.

    b You can usually enjoy a sexy joke with him/her.

    c Even in the most serious situations you can share a laugh.

24 If you are having a moan to your lover, how does he/she respond?

    a You don't dare complain in case he/she gets bored with you.

    b He/she says you are a dreadful nag and usually goes out.

    c He/she listens attentively and tries to put things right.

25 You fly into a temper because you're feeling tired. How does your lover react?

    a He/she threatens to leave you if you behave irrationally.

    b He/she rants and rages back at you.

    c With good-natured patience and sympathy.

26 If you had a big problem you would:

    a Keep it to yourself for fear of an angry rebuke from your lover.

    b Know it would not interest your lover.

    c Try to solve it by discussing it at length with your lover.

27 Does your lover pay attention when you talk to him/her?

    a Practically everything you say goes 'in one ear, and out the other'.

    b If you shout loud enough he/she will listen.

    c You are his/her favourite person for conversation.

28 You are in the bathroom with the door closed. Your lover would:

    a Barge in without knocking.

    b Bang on the door and demand to know what you are doing.

    c Respect your privacy and leave you alone.

29 Do you sometimes feel your sex life is so stale you would both be better off with someone else?

    a There are times when your lover makes you feel like an object.

    b Whatever else goes wrong, your sex life is pretty good with your lover.

c Of course, sex, like anything else, cannot always be perfect, but you can't think of anyone other than your lover you would rather be with.

30   A picnic in the country with your lover usually means:

  a Hard work for you.
  b Driving around to find a heavily populated spot.
  c A time to enjoy each other.

31   Are you disappointed with the way things have worked out between you and your lover?

  a If only he/she could be the way they were when you first met – he/she used to be so charming.
  b If he/she could keep control of his/her 'roving eye' you could be good pals.
  c You can't think how he/she could endear him/herself more to you.

32   Which attributes do you value most in your lover?

  a Kindness to dumb animals.
  b Good looks and figure.
  c A warm heart and generous spirit.

33   A letter arrives for you from a foreign country. Your lover would:

  a Rip it open and read it without your permission.
  b Stand over you while you tried to read it.
  c Leave you to open it in peace and let you decide whether you wish to discuss the contents.

34   When your lover is sexually satisfied he/she:

  a Turns over and falls asleep.
  b Suggests you go elsewhere if you haven't had enough.
  c Ensures your satisfaction too.

35   Under what circumstances would your lover give you a massage?

  a Never, he/she prefers being on the receiving end of a massage.
  b If he/she thought it was turning on someone watching whom he/she fancied.

c Often, as a prelude to love-making or just to give you relaxing pleasure.

36 On your birthday or anniversary, your lover would:

a Forget the date and have to be reminded by you.

b Take you for a meal where he/she knew he/she could be the centre of attention.

c Always surprise you with an imaginative gift or outing.

37 Arriving very late for a date with you in a restaurant, your lover would:

a Demand to know why you had not ordered.

b Probably find you chatting up the waiter/waitress.

c Apologise profusely and do his/her best to make amends.

38 On a long plane journey a very attractive traveller occupies the seat next to your partner. Your partner would:

a Pretend he/she was someone very important and infer that you were only along for the ride.

b Spend the entire journey chatting up the stranger.

c Be friendly to the stranger and introduce you as his/her partner.

39 You have been having an extremely busy week at work. Your lover:

a Arrives home with a crowd of people, expecting you to entertain them.

b Gets petulant if you are not inclined to go to a party.

c Shows you every consideration and has a delicious meal ready for you.

40 Does your lover go to great lengths to seduce you?

a Hardly, he/she thinks you are there for the taking – as and when he/she wants.

b He/she has a pretty polished seduction routine.

c There is no need – wanting you is a sufficient turn-on.

SCORING

Each question allowed you to give one of three answers, marked 'a', 'b' and 'c'. Add up the number of 'a', 'b' and 'c' responses you gave separately – this will give you three scores out of 40. Look at the relative size of these three scores and interpret them as follows:

Mostly 'a's

You are probably very insecure in your relationship and unsure about the character of your partner. That is not surprising since it appears from the outside point of view that he/she treats you very badly indeed. Can it be that you do not realise this and think his/her behaviour is quite normal for a long-term partner? This is most likely not the case – the pattern of your replies suggests that you have a pretty good idea that your partner behaves in a way that is selfish, inconsiderate and unloving.

This naturally raises the question of why you tolerate this person – why you are still with them. Is it that you are about to break up and the results of this quiz are no more than confirmation of the need to go ahead and do so? Or could it be that you feel trapped in the relationship in some way. Perhaps you lack confidence in yourself and think, rightly or wrongly, that you will not be able to attract anyone else at all – let alone somebody who would treat you with greater love and respect. It cannot be guaranteed that you would be able to do better than your current partner but you could not do worse, and you might reflect upon the possibility that you would be happier living alone than devoting yourself to another person who cares so little for you and treats you as little better than dirt.

You may be married to this person already and caught up in all the commitments that marriage entails – children, shared property, relatives, etc. If there are sound practical reasons for your reluctance to disband the relationship, you could perhaps try some marriage counselling – first alone, and then hopefully persuading your partner to accompany you. Sometimes an outsider's point of view can provide new insights which would help your partner to love, or at least behave towards you, better. Failing that, you could at least leave your answers to this quiz lying around where he/she is likely to find them, in case this helps them see things from your point of view.

Mostly 'b's

You and your lover certainly have a passionate and volatile relationship. The fact that it is based on sex is not necessarily a bad thing – as long as you do not decide you would like to settle down to a more comfortable, conventional lifestyle. Life is just a big sexual play-pen to your lover who seems to be constantly seeking new exciting outlets for his/her high libido.

Could it be that your partner is extremely young and wants to play the field before finally making a nest? This is all very well, but you should consider that, with all the variety around, you may not be the bird who eventually helps him/her feather the nest. On the other hand, he/she may be going through some kind of mid-life crisis, in need of reassurance of his/her attractiveness and sexual potency. Your inability to trust your lover out of your sight may well be justified, but while he/she is going through this phase, it is doubtful that you can do much to change him/her. Acting on the defensive all the time will not help; you need to make it clear in what ways you are hurt by your lover's behaviour.

It may be that you are something of a fun-loving swinger yourself, in which case there is no real problem. If, however, your flirtatious behaviour is motivated mainly by a need to retaliate and give your partner a taste of his/her own medicine, then there is a danger that mutual jealousies could spiral out of control. In any case, it is improper to use the affections of other people as pawns in some game of political chess you are playing against your lover.

Mostly 'c's

Yours seems to be a healthy, complete relationship in which your partner treats you with great love and consideration. Your mutual intimacy, trust and communication is something that most people can only envy and try to emulate. No doubt your lover is a beautiful person, but I cannot help suspecting that your own behaviour towards him/her is a major factor in the equation. The whole world loves a lover and it is to be hoped that your mutual happiness will continue long into the future.

The chemistry of scores

If you have previously completed and scored the quiz to assess how good a lover *you* are (Chapter 18), you might find it interesting to compare your own scores with those of your lover.

If, for example, you both came out with mostly '**a**'s, then it could be said that you deserve each other. Alternatively, you may both be perfectly nice people as individuals, but your relationship has spiralled downwards so that you no longer give each other 'strokes', physical or emotional. Whether you treat your partner badly because of the way he/she treats you, or vice versa, is a chicken and egg problem with no easy solution, and probably matters little anyway at this stage of proceedings.

If you are a dreamy, romantic '**b**' scorer and your partner is anything but a '**c**', then you are probably surviving on your fantasy. This is fine until the bubble bursts, as some day it is bound to.

If both of you are '**c**'s, this is the ideal and you may be assured of a long and happy future.

If your partner is a '**c**' and you are something else, consider well what you stand to lose and how likely you are to do so if you carry on with your current mode of behaviour.

20

HOW WELL ARE YOU

COMMUNICATING?

Surveys on marital happiness repeatedly point to the importance of communication within a relationship. Asked what caused the breakdown of their marriage, most people will cite reasons such as adultery, cruelty, neglect or sexual incompatibility, but these are frequently just symptoms of a lack of communication between couples.

But what exactly is communication? Difficulties in agreeing about the meaning of the word arise from the fact that it has at least two aspects: the first is the ability to express one's true feelings to the partner, whether directly through words or indirectly through body language. This implies a capacity to send clear messages rather than signals that are irrelevant, ambiguous, misdirected or otherwise confused. It is no good, for example, being angry with your partner, if it is really someone else, such as your mother, who is responsible for upsetting you. Equally, there is little point in taking it out on the children, the cat, or the milkman if you are really annoyed with your spouse.

The attempt to bottle up strongly felt emotion so that it is not expressed at all is also unhelpful. In fact, it is usually impossible; emotions such as anger and anxiety, if not expressed, have a way of manifesting themselves through physical and mental symptoms such as ulcers, asthma, high blood pressure, heart disease, alcoholism, depression, possibly even cancer.

In recent decades, assertiveness training has become very popular and one of the key aspects of this is learning how to express feelings to other people. Americans, especially, are often heard to inform each other explicitly in terms such as these: 'Your refusal to help with the washing up makes me feel angry and resentful.' 'I feel anxious and jealous when you go away on weekend business trips.' 'I am feeling deprived of affection and sexually frustrated because we have not made love in two weeks.' While statements such as these may seem crude, forward and egocentric to discreet British ears, one wonders if the recent decline in stress-related diseases in America (compared with increasing levels in Britain), recently reported by Professor Cary Cooper of Manchester Institute of Technology, could be partly due to this new-found openness of emotional expression.

A second aspect of communication is the amount of understanding shown by the partner. After all, it is no good transmitting clear messages unless the apparatus for receiving them is intact and functioning. However much you express your thoughts and feelings to your partner you will not get through to him/her if he/she is completely indifferent to your well-being or actively resistant to the message you are trying to put across. For example, you would have little joy in communicating your distress at your partner's continual late night arrivals if he/she is having an ecstatic affair with someone else and has no intention of changing the status quo. He/she simply would not want to listen. Communication in a partnership therefore involves being in tune with each other – understanding as well as expressing.

The importance of communication in marriage was highlighted in a survey conducted some years ago by Dr R. J. Burke and colleagues at York University. Nearly 200 couples were asked how likely they were to disclose unpleasant and distressing feelings to their spouse. The findings showed that wives were more likely to disclose their feelings than husbands, and couples with happy marriages were more likely to discuss their problems than unhappy couples.

Husbands and wives gave similar reasons for disclosing problems to their spouses, most commonly 'unburdening' or 'catharsis', the seeking of solutions, advice, clarification, new perspectives, emotional support or enhancement of mutual understanding. Wives who withheld feelings did so because they did not want to burden or worry their husband, who had enough on his mind already, or because they thought it would be a waste of time – he would be unresponsive to their problems anyway. Non-disclosing husbands said they preferred to separate work from home, or felt that their wife lacked knowledge necessary to appreciate their difficulties.

Asked how they would like their spouse to change, the wives wanted their husbands to be more responsive and receptive to their problems, while husbands wished their wives would react to their problems less hysterically so as not to add further stress.

Thus it seems that there are individual differences in preferred modes of communication and some average differences between men and women. All the cartoons depicting nagging wives and husbands who hide behind the newspaper at breakfast seem to reflect a certain truth. These differences could well be at the root of a great deal of marital stress. Most of us need to share our inner feelings with someone, and it is certainly ideal if we feel free and inclined to do this with the person we live and sleep with.

Other research by Burke and colleagues has shown that wives are not only more expressive than husbands, but more sensitive to the emotional states of their husband – thus confirming the stereotype of the wife as intuitive and supportive. However, this wifely empathy was found to decline markedly if the wife was working or following the appearance of children (presumably because these things compete for a woman's energy and attention).

Psychologists at Iowa State University, USA, led by Dr D. G. Dean, reasoned that if couples were communicating properly, they would be able to make accurate guesses concerning each other's likes and dislikes. In particular, they chose to study colour preferences for items such as cars, telephones and living-room walls. Each individual was asked to choose colours for these articles and then guess which colour his/her spouse would choose. The discrepancy between actual choices and spouses' predictions was found to relate quite strongly to marital happiness. This technique for gauging to what extent a couple are in tune with each other was the basis of a popular TV game show (called 'Mr and Mrs' in Britain) and readers may find it interesting to try it out for themselves.

Clearly, the ability to communicate effectively within a partnership is of major importance. Inability to understand the other's point of view, or be understood by them, whether on matters emotional or intellectual, whether in the bedroom or in general, is bound to erode the happiness of a relationship in the long term. To find out how well you are communicating in your relationship answer the 40 questions below.

I You want to make love. How do you indicate this to your partner?

   a By touching and speaking to them in a seductive way.
   b Tell them in a straightforward manner.
   c Complain that you hardly ever have sex.

2 At a boring dinner party, you want to leave early. You:

   a Remind your partner of an imaginary early start in the morning.

b Drum your fingers on the table and give knowing looks to your partner.

c Yawn loudly and pull a sulky face.

3 You get sore during love-making – how do you tell your lover?

a Talk it over in a less heated moment of passion, to find a solution.

b Blurt it out as soon as he/she has finished.

c Yell when he/she touches you.

4 What gesture do you use to show affection to your lover?

a A special little signal that you share only with each other.

b A hearty squeeze.

c A pat on the head that you otherwise reserve for the family pet.

5 You are woken from sleep by your partner urgently pressing up against your body. You:

a Succumb to their caress and dreamily make love.

b Mumble grumpily that they can go ahead as long as you are not disturbed.

c Protest angrily and drag off the duvet to sleep on the sofa.

6 Your partner asks your opinion of a meal he/she has prepared for you. You:

a Say it is delicious and praise his/her efforts.

b Tell the truth at all costs.

c Say it would probably have been cheaper to eat out.

7 You are somewhat distressed that your partner climbs into bed without washing first. You:

a Make a sexy ritual out of bathing him/her late at night.

b Point out that natural body odours are not always the greatest turn-on.

c Pointedly spray air freshener in the bedroom last thing at night.

8 A bad day makes you snappy with your lover. You would:

a Apologise quickly and explain your ill-humour.

b Tell a joke to relieve the tension.

c Leave him/her to suffer since he/she does the same to you.

9 Your partner continually just misses touching the spot which gives you the most pleasure during sex. You:

a Invent a fantasy in which you describe the pleasure the characters receive when touched in a certain way.

b Grab his/her hand and put it on the place.

c Get frustrated and irritable with him/her.

10 You say something really hurtful to your lover just as he/she is leaving for work. You would:

a Ring them and apologise for being so horrid.

b Leave a sorry note for his/her return home.

c Dismiss him/her as being over-sensitive.

11 What would you do if your partner was repeatedly just failing to give you satisfaction during love-making?

a Tell him/her how to satisfy you.

b Buy a vibrator to top up afterwards.

c Avoid sex as much as possible.

12 A good time to discuss an important issue with your lover is:

a In bed at night.

b Over the kitchen table at breakfast.

c The minute he/she walks in the door from work.

13 Your partner suffers from flatulence. You:

a Attempt to modify his/her diet.

b Leave a bottle of charcoal pills in a prominent place.

c Sleep in another room.

14 You most often greet your partner with:

a A kiss and a smile.

b A few words of greeting.

c A list of chores that need doing.

15 When you are making love you:

a Often whisper little fantasies to your lover.

b 'Talk dirty' if he/she requires it.

c Always do so in complete silence.

16 You influence your partner by:

a Gentle persuasion.

b Stubborn determination.

c Shouting the loudest.

17 Your partner will usually do as you ask because:

a He/she adores you.

b He/she is a bit frightened of you.

c You have the strongest will.

18 You can heal aches and pains in your lover by:

a Lovingly applied massage with warm oils.

b An effective analgesic.

c Saying his/her favourite film is on at the local cinema.

19 When your lover faces a disappointment he/she knows you will respond with:

a A big hug and a shoulder to cry on.

b Embarrassment.

c Remonstrations concerning his/her failure.

20 How often do you express your feelings for your partner?

a There are literally dozens of ways, in words and actions, that you show your love for him/her.

b You try to remember to be nice.

c You cannot express emotion easily.

21 Discussing your relationship with your partner you:

a Constructively deal with any problems you may have together.

b Discover you can't always get through to him/her.

c Want to bang his/her head to make him/her see reason.

22 You suspect your lover of being unfaithful to you. You:

a Enquire in a gentle, teasing way whether it is true.

b Come straight out with your suspicions and demand an answer.

c Keep nagging and taxing him/her until he/she clams up completely.

23 When you do something stupid, like locking yourself out of the house, what do you do?

a Tell your lover what an idiot you've been.

b Swear, bang the door and lose your temper generally.

c Blame your lover for distracting your attention and causing you to forget your keys.

24 What do you talk about mostly when you are alone with your lover?

    a Anything and everything.

    b The direction your relationship is heading.

    c Domestic matters and monetary problems.

25 If you have been watching a TV play or documentary together, what happens afterwards?

    a You both voice your opinions even if you don't agree.

    b You try to avoid a discussion since you already know his/her viewpoint.

    c You seldom enjoy watching the same type of programme.

26 Your partner has a habit, such as smoking, which you loathe. You would:

    a Tell him/her how happy it would make you if he/she could give it up.

    b Threaten him/her with dire consequences if he/she continues.

    c Flush his/her cigarettes down the toilet.

27 Most of your disagreements occur over:

    a Small matters easily resolved.

    b Money.

    c Basic misunderstandings.

28 Your partner reveals a rather personal quirk of yours at a party. You:

    a Laugh it off, knowing it was not meant maliciously.

    b Tell him/her off soundly.

    c Spill the beans about all his/her funny little habits.

29 You are in a different room and your lover calls you. Do you:

    a Go to see what he/she wants.

    b Call back 'just a minute'.

    c Pretend you have not heard.

30   Do you criticise your lover's sexual performance?

    a You would not dream of destroying his/her confidence.
    b If you can back up your criticism with a useful comment.
    c You seek revenge for his/her criticism of you.

31   What do you do when your love-making is so predictable it becomes boring?

    a You would never let things get to that stage.
    b Ask your lover to tell you if it is your fault.
    c Say something icy when your lover goes to touch you.

32   Your partner tells you he/she doesn't like the way you are dressed just before you are going out together. You:

    a Would take it as a constructive remark and change.
    b Get flustered and upset.
    c Make a sarcastic remark back about the way he/she looks.

33   Navigating new territory, your partner, who is driving, takes a wrong turn. You:

    a Get out the map and trace a new route.
    b Pretend not to notice you are going the wrong way.
    c Sit back smugly and tell him/her what a fool he/she is.

34   On your birthday, your lover buys you something you don't like. You:

    a Thank them for the gift and comment on his/her general kindness.
    b Tell him/her honestly the damaging truth.
    c Say it's about time he/she knew what you wanted.

35   In an intimate moment, your lover confesses that he/she is very unsure of him/herself. You:

    a Build his/her self-confidence in every possible way.
    b Use it against him/her when you are next having a row.
    c Cannot bear weakness in other people.

36   Your partner is more experienced than you sexually. You are:

    a A willing and eager pupil.
    b Too proud to admit there are aspects of sex on which you are not very knowledgeable.
    c Reluctant to have your lover 'experiment' on you.

37 A candlelit dinner in a restaurant with your partner is a time when:

    a You can relax and get sexy with each other.
    b You unload all your problems on to him/her.
    c You find you have nothing to talk about.

38 You stay with your partner because:

    a You make each other extremely happy.
    b You've grown on each other like a habit.
    c You are 'trapped' in a situation from which you can't escape.

39 Your partner is away and an urgent decision needs to be made which affects both of you. You would:

    a Be pretty sure that he/she would agree with your decision.
    b Worry about what to do.
    c Decide on what suits you best and too bad if he/she doesn't like it.

40 Your partner tries to tell you his/her troubles. You:

    a Listen attentively and try to help.
    b Get a glazed look in your eyes and pick up a newspaper to read.
    c Think he/she has a nerve – with all you have to cope with.

SCORING

Give yourself 3 points for each 'a' answer, 2 points for each 'b', and 1 point for each 'c'. This will give you a total score varying from 40 to 120.

Score: 100–120

Excellent. You appear to have a very warm and effective level of communication with your partner and the betting is that your relationship is a very happy and comfortable one. You give the right social and emotional strokes and at the same time you know when it is best to withhold your advice and information because it might be intrusive.

Score: 80–99

Reasonable. Yours is a fairly typical relationship; for the most part you understand and empathise with each other, but there are occasional lapses (probably on both sides) and these lead to slight misunderstandings. You do not necessarily need to talk more – it could just be a matter of choosing the right moment to say things and the right tone of voice. Remember that sometimes a degree of warmth and subtlety is necessary to make an idea palatable to others. Honesty may be a virtue, but bluntness can sometimes be hurtful.

Score: 60–79

Less than satisfactory. Your communication is slightly deficient and you should consider how your relationship might be rebuilt by giving more consideration to it. Basically, the skill you need to learn is how to express your thoughts and feelings in such a way as not to antagonise your partner. Telling a person directly and explicitly why you are upset by him/her may put him/her on the defensive and reduce the likelihood that he/she will respond constructively.

Score: 40–59

Disastrous. It appears that your relationship may already have broken down beyond repair – that is, unless it is the mutual hostility and distaste for one another that you find entertaining and which motivates you to continue. Probably this will come as no surprise to you – you have been aware of the cold war for a long time and this quiz has only served to confirm and quantify it. If not, and you would really like things to improve, then you would be well advised to seek the help of a marriage counsellor.

Analysing your skills

Assuming your performance was less than perfect, you may find it instructive to go back over the quiz questions to see where you 'went wrong' and how your behaviour might be modified so as to enhance your relationship. To some extent, it is true, the 'ideal' answers are a matter of opinion. Sometimes the author's choices could be backed up by scientific studies, but in other instances they are based on intuition. The reader is therefore free to disagree with the scoring values, though it may help to explain the criteria used.

'a' answers usually reflect a communication pattern that is considerate as well as expressive. People responding in this way are usually effective in informing and persuading their partners because they adopt an approach that is subtle and gentle besides being warm and loving. They recognise that there are times when it is best not to confront the partner with truths that are certain to be hurtful and unlikely to be helpful. It may thus come as a surprise to readers to realise that direct expressions of thoughts and feelings do not always rate top in the scoring.

An example is the item concerning reactions to a meal your partner has cooked which you did not enjoy (Question 6). In this case, notifying him/her of your taste likes and dislikes should take second place to your appreciation of his/her efforts to please you. It is not so much a matter of telling white lies as focusing praise on what is good in the situation. Putting it another way, feelings may be just as true as facts.

'b' answers usually imply a willingness to communicate but an inability to do it right. Sometimes there is disclosure which is too direct, too explicit, too aggressive. For example, the person who announces that he/she wants to make love immediately (Question 1) may catch his/her partner ill-prepared and unsure of his/her ability to respond with full warmth. The intention may be admirable, but the execution slightly clumsy.

In other cases, the 'b' answer may be slightly oblique, or even irrelevant, to what is really called for in the situation. For example, upon realising that you have misdirected your anger to your partner when he/she was not deserving of it (Question 8), the correct thing to do is to apologise directly, not try to redress the balance by being subsequently nicer than you would otherwise have been. Thus 'b' answers are not particularly destructive but they fall short of perfection in various ways.

'c' answers are characteristically cold, hostile, selfish and hurtful, and there is little more that can be said about them. They are almost invariably symptomatic of a relationship that is already on the rocks, and if they are to have any effect at all it is likely to be one of smashing the wreckage around even more. They are counterproductive rather than constructive, and the bitter, resentful, vengeful element to many of these responses suggests retaliation for similar treatment from the partner. Who fired the first icicle in the cold war may be as difficult to determine as whether the chicken or egg has priority.

About the author

Dr Glenn Wilson is Senior Lecturer at the University of London and one of Britain's best known psychologists. An expert on personality, love, sexual behaviour and psychology of performance, he has published more than 100 scientific articles and 25 books, including *The Psychology of Sex, Love and Instinct, Variant Psychology: Research and Theory, The Great Sex Divide,* and *Psychology for Performing Artists: Butterflies and Bouquets.* He makes frequent radio and TV appearances and has lectured widely abroad, holding visiting appointments at California State University, Los Angeles, Stanford University and the University of Nevada, Reno.